Woman's Day Gifts from Your Kitchen

Woman's Day Gifts from Your Kitchen

Illustrated by JOHN TROTTA

Gramercy Publishing Company
New York

This 1982 edition is published by Gramercy Publishing
Company distributed by Crown Publishers, Inc. by
arrangement with CBS Publications, The Consumer
Publishing Division of CBS Inc.

Manufactured in the United States of America

Library of Congress Cataloging in Publication Data

Woman's day gifts from your kitchen.

  Includes index.
  1. Cookery.   2. Gifts.   I. Woman's day.   II. Title:
Gifts from your kitchen.
TX652.W68   1982   641.8   82-6106
                                           AACR2

ISBN: 0-517-386003

h g f e d c b a

Contents

Introduction

A GIFT that you make yourself is very special because part of *you* is in it, a generous sampling of your time, your effort and your love. And when a homemade gift is a gift from your kitchen—beautiful to look at, delicious to eat, made with the best ingredients—you have the added pleasure of sharing satisfying, wholesome nourishment with your family and your friends.

Woman's Day *Gifts from Your Kitchen* is much more than a collection of wonderful recipes for delicious gift foods. It is meant to inspire you by showing how exciting it is to create original gifts that express your own personality. It will encourage you to make thrifty use of nature's bounty, from season to season, for gifts you can give as you make them or store in your very own "gift shop"—a freezer and pantry full of sumptuous, homemade treasures. Of course, you can also use this book only occasionally, when you want to make a splendid gift of food for someone very dear to you. But we hope that these recipes will become an important part of your everyday life as well as your gift-giving.

Whether you make a tangy cheese spread, a crusty loaf of whole-grain bread, crisp cookies, or gleaming fruit jellies, each gift of homemade food is unique because every cook will add her own special touches to the recipe. Your cake layers may be a little higher on one side or decorations may vary from cookie to cookie, but these small imperfections or variations only add to the charm of the gift.

And it goes without saying that homemade foods almost always taste better than those you buy in a store. Because they are made in small batches with just the right ingredients, they have full fresh flavor. Cakes have a special lightness. Breads are full of old-fashioned goodness. If you make Sour Rye Bread, for example, you start with nourishing whole-rye flour, add pure molasses and other high-quality ingredients, and the result is a rich-tasting very special home-baked loaf.

Baking cookies, kneading bread dough, boiling up candy syrups, putting up pickles—these are satisfying, homespun activities, which bring back memories of Grandma's kitchen, of the warmth and closeness that comes from sharing simple pleasures. Everyone in the family is usually willing to do this kind of work because the preparations are such fun and the results are so delectable. We know many families who have annual cookie baking days at Christmastime and Easter cake-baking sessions to make beautiful layer cakes or cupcakes with colored icings and candied flowers. Very often the children of the family are the most imaginative and creative gift-makers, and decorating cookies and cakes is a favorite job. It's great fun to create individual and unusual decorations, and there's the added reward of getting to scrape the bowl.

And there are others who might like to share the fun. Perhaps you and a neighbor could join forces to make special preserves and relishes when the garden produce is at its height, or turn out big batches of Fruited Cheese Logs, Spiced Almonds or Wine Jelly for holiday gift-giving. If you team up with her for a day in the kitchen, you'll not only enjoy each other's company, but you'll find many ways to make the whole process more efficient. You could get together with a friend to plan your gift lists early and then shop together for wrappings and imaginative containers. If you do things with a friend, you're much more likely to do it on time and to enjoy it more.

It's also a pleasure to think of all the money to be saved, "putting by" the flavorful vegetables and fruits that you have grown in your own garden or bought in season. If you don't have a garden of your own, it's worth a trip to a country farm stand to buy large quantities of things that you can cook, freeze, preserve and store. Try to keep in tune with the seasons and you will find there is a natural rhythm that helps to keep things in balance. If you boil up jams and jellies when fruits and berries are ripe and juicy, if you pickle, can and freeze summer vegetables when they are in lush abundance, if you make candy and cookies on crisp winter days when they are easiest to handle, and if you bake and freeze breads and cakes whenever you feel like it and have the time, you will always have lots of things to give from a supply that is continually being replenished. And how wonderfully comforting it is to know that your pantry shelves are lined with glistening jars of homemade pickles, relishes, jams and seasonings, with containers of luscious candies and other little goodies, and that your freezer is stocked with wholesome homebaked breads, cakes and cookies. It's like having a lot of money in the bank.

Even if your schedule is too hectic to allow time for making preserves, pickles and other good things that keep well over long periods, you'll find wonderful recipes for gifts from your kitchen that can be made in a hurry and given soon after. However, if giving from your kitchen becomes a way of life, chances are you'll have something on hand for any occasion, regardless of the time of year.

Selecting a Gift of Food

We have chosen a wide variety of recipes to delight friends of all ages and tastes and to greet every festive occasion. There are formal gifts for weddings, birthdays, anniversaries and graduations and gifts for special holidays like Easter, Christmas and Thanksgiving. There are gifts to bring to a sick friend, to your dinner-party hostess, to a new neighbor. There are gifts to send to a child at camp, to a distant relative, to the folks back home. There are gifts to give for no reason at all, except to say that you are thinking of someone and want to bring them enjoyment.

Choosing just the right thing for the person you have in mind is much easier when you can make it yourself. You can delight a chocolate-lover with three different kinds of chocolate cookies, or a friend who loves Indian food with two different chutneys.

A loaf of Cranberry Whole-Wheat Bread or a Cinnamon Loaf might be just the thing for a weekend hostess or you could bring her a very special salad dressing in a handsome cruet —this would be especially good in the summer. Kids will welcome Peanut-Butter Chocolate, Popcorn Balls, or Cereal-Peanut Crisp. And why not give the traditional Christmas dessert of English Plum Pudding to several friends this year. The homemade kind is superb—straight out of Dickens! It's much more fun to give good things from your kitchen than other gifts and it's much more practical.

Planning is essential for successful gifts of food. Most pies should be given when they are fresh; *don't* plan to make a gift pie in the midst of Christmas preparations when you will be swamped with so many chores; *do* make it ahead and freeze it when you are not so busy, if you can. If you plan to send a gift of food by mail, choose something that keeps well, can be packed conveniently and will not easily break. Such perishables as Herb Butter and Custard Sauce must be kept in the refrigerator; don't plan to bring them on a lengthy car trip, especially in hot weather, unless you have a cooler in which to carry them.

Decorating a Gift of Food

Food that looks good seems to taste better. Your friends won't know how delicious your gift is until they actually eat it, but you can show them that it's special by the way you decorate and present it. Your gift of food should be beautiful to see; give it with some ceremony and with unconcealed pride.

Decorate cookies and cakes with colored icings or glazes, or garnish them with nuts, raisins, dried fruits, berries, candies, sprinkles or colored sugars. Make cookies in special shapes to suit the occasion: bunnies and eggs for Easter, witches and pumpkins for Halloween. You can personalize a cake by writing a funny or serious message on it with tinted icing, or by decorating it with fresh or candied flowers, flags or miniature toys of some special significance. For a friend who is leaving on a trip, arrange a single layer of Bourbon Brownies in a shallow box and write "Bon Voyage" on them in colored icing, one letter to a square. Decorate Christmas breads with candied green pineapple and red cherries, or with evergreen sprigs and red berries. Trim Christmas cookies and cakes with red- and green-tinted sugar or coconut, tiny candy canes, red cinnamon candies or gumdrops.

Selecting Wrappings and Containers

Get in the habit of saving things that will make good wrappings or containers for your gifts. Keep a carton handy and fill it with things you want to use: bits of used wrapping paper and of self-adhesive shelf-lining paper, wallpaper samples, tissue paper from dress boxes, yarn, ribbon, lace, velvet and cotton fabrics, attractive posters, newspapers with amusing or dramatic headlines. Notary seals and large gold stars make good labels, or you can cut out designs with open centers from magazines or wrapping paper and use double-faced masking tape to attach them as labels.

Collect jars, bottles, boxes and tins that have interesting shapes and colors. Plastic berry boxes, woven with checked ribbon or lined with bright tissue paper, make excellent containers for snacks and candies, as do the coffee, shortening and nut cans that come with plastic lids. Save any container that is attractive and will be roomy enough to show the food off properly. Jewel-tone vinegars, jams and jellies, for example, look beautiful in glass jars and bottles that expose their lovely colors to the light.

Use your imagination to fashion containers for the foods you've made. Paint coffee cans or decorate them with cutouts of self-adhesive paper. Decorate paper plates and napkins with felt-tipped pens and use them to wrap cookies and cake squares. A hand-decorated hatbox makes a fine container for a layer cake. If you have the time and facilities, you might try making more elaborate containers: a wooden box, a bread board, a basket or a clay pot. Children often can be enlisted to make boxes, cannisters and pots, either at home or in the school shop.

You can also buy inexpensive items to use as containers for gifts of food. Buy things when you see them in five-and-ten-cent stores, supermarkets, drugstores, hardware stores, at barn or rummage sales and in thrift shops. There is a wide range of objects that will suit your needs.

Seasoned butters, cheese spreads, special mustards and relishes can be packed into plastic cups, pottery crocks, tiny soufflé dishes, custard cups, small copper molds, glass measuring cups or pretty coffee mugs. Sauces and dressings look good in ceramic or clear glass wine and vinegar bottles or in glass cruets. Candies, nuts and snacks are charming in decorated coffee or nut cans, in wooden or metal boxes, in a candy or nut dish, a glass jar, a brandy snifter or even an ice bucket.

Pack herb mixtures into plastic bags tied with a ribbon or in spice jars or a mortar; mustards in mustard pots; relishes in canning jars or on a relish tray; jellies and jams in jelly jars or in a lidded jam dish with a spoon. Give bread on a bread board or in a breadbox or baking pan; pies in glass, pottery or china pie plates; cakes on decorated paper plates, a pretty platter or tray or in a round, shallow basket. Delicate cakes travel best in a bakery-store cakebox or a hatbox, either of which can be decorated with cutouts or with paints.

Desserts look wonderful in glass or ceramic jars, in a soufflé dish or mold, in a baking dish or in a small glass fishbowl. You can divide desserts, if you wish, into individual portions and pack them in plastic cups, custard cups or tiny soufflé dishes.

Cookies and candies keep best in pretty tins or hand-decorated shortening or coffee cans. Try using seasonal ornaments such as pine or spruce twigs, dried leaves or flowers, hearts, doilies or old photographs to decorate cans and tins. Cookies also look great in tall apothecary jars, or you can wrap them in plastic bags or arrange them on decorated paper plates covered with clear plastic. Or pack cookies in a large mixing bowl, a useful gift in itself.

Small candies and other snacks will look pretty in a new

flowerpot, a vase or a brandy snifter. Candies for children are a great hit when they are packed in a plastic pail, a watering can, a lunchbox, a dump truck or some other attractive toy. Little girls will be delighted with a straw pocketbook or basket filled with foil-wrapped candies.

Including Useful Accessories

Many of the containers that we have suggested are gifts in themselves that will last long after the food is gone, a pleasant reminder of your thoughtfulness. You can also buy accessories to include with your gift of food, things that are useful, attractive additions to any kitchen. A good serrated bread knife or a pretty butter spreader nicely complement a gift of bread. A cheese board or a cheese slicer go well with a cheese spread, a rolling pin with pie, a cake server or flour sifter with a cake, a candy thermometer with candy. Such accessories need not be expensive: give a wooden spoon or some cookie cutters with cookies, a wire whisk with a dessert or a basting brush with a sauce.

Choosing Companion Foods

You can also give several homemade foods that go well with each other: Oatmeal Bread with Pear Honey, for example, or Croissants with Herb Butter. Plain cakes like Sour-Cream Pound Cake go well with special sauces like Russian Apricot Sauce or Brandy Custard Sauce. Making up your own combinations is one of the great pleasures in giving food.

You can also buy certain foods to accompany what you've made: a box of fine, imported biscuits with a homemade cheese spread, a large, beautiful melon with a special dessert sauce, a jar of coffee beans with a coffee cake or some imported tea with a pound cake.

Giving Recipes and Suggestions

You may wish to include serving suggestions with your gift: "Keep refrigerated" or "Serve at room temperature over vanilla pudding or plain cake." Type, print or write such instructions neatly on a tag or card that you have decorated with crayons or paints and attach to the gift.

Including the recipe with the food that you are giving is a nice touch, especially if you are giving it to someone who likes to cook and bake. If the recipe calls for a somewhat unusual or appealing ingredient—rye flour, cinnamon sticks, vanilla beans, hazelnuts, dried fruits—you can also give that ingredient along with the gift and the recipe. Write the recipe on a recipe card and sign your name and the date at the bottom. In this way, your gift of food will become a permanent one, for someone will think of you fondly each time your recipe is used.

Let giving from your kitchen become part of your way of life and your gifts a happy and generous expression of your love. Once you begin to live this way, you'll find it hard to stop, not only because you'll enjoy it so much, but because your family and friends will begin to look forward to your wonderful gifts. They won't settle for less, nor will you.

Giving in this way ultimately becomes a very personal experience. Woman's Day *Gifts from Your Kitchen* will set you on your way.

Appetizers and Snacks

A T HOLIDAY GATHERINGS, big cocktail parties or small dinner parties, special appetizers and snacks add a note of welcome and hospitality. In this section we have gathered together a rich variety of cheese spreads, easy pâtés, seasoned nuts, and other goodies that are irresistible to nibblers. Give them for holidays, to a weekend hostess, or present them to a friend who is just about to give her annual big bash. These treats are welcome any time.

Ideas for Giving Appetizers or Snacks

The nicest way to give any of these delicious foods is to put them in an imaginative container that will be useful later. Cheese spreads look good in pottery crocks or a small glass bowl or a small soufflé dish. You could also pack them in small copper molds, a glass measuring cup or a pretty mug. Include a spreader or cheese knife, if you wish, or a box or two of imported biscuits.

Pack seasoned nuts in painted coffee, shortening or nut cans with plastic lids, in handsome small wooden or metal boxes, in a pretty ceramic dish, a glass jar or brandy snifter. Olives look especially appealing in clear glass containers—try glass canning jars or nicely shaped bottles.

DOUBLE-CHEESE CROCK

8 ounces sharp Cheddar,
  Swiss or Jack cheese,
  coarsely shredded
4 ounces Mozzarella or any
  mild cheese, coarsely
  shredded
¼ cup butter or margarine,
  softened

1 tablespoon brandy, sherry,
  port wine or beer
½ cup finely chopped nuts or
  2 teaspoons lightly
  crushed caraway seeds

Beat the cheeses, butter and brandy in a mixing bowl until well blended; fold in the nuts or seeds. Pack into a container or ceramic crock, cover and refrigerate about 1 week before giving. Suggest serving with crackers or crisp cut-up vegetables. *Makes about 1½ cups.*

CEREAL-CHEESE SQUARES

1 cup coarsely shredded
  sharp Cheddar cheese,
  at room temperature
½ cup margarine, at room
  temperature

1 cup crisp rice cereal
1 cup flour
⅛ teaspoon salt
½ teaspoon hot pepper sauce

Preheat the oven to 350° F.

Combine the cheese, margarine, cereal, flour, salt and pepper sauce in a bowl and mix thoroughly. Turn out onto a very lightly floured board and pat or roll into a rectangle 6 by 8 inches and about ⅜ inch thick. Using a ruler, cut with a knife into 1-inch squares. Place each square carefully, 2 inches apart, on a lightly greased baking sheet. Bake 15 to 20 minutes, or until lightly browned. Cool on rack. Store airtight. Give in ice-cube trays wrapped in tissue paper or cellophane. *Makes 4 dozen.*

FRUITED CHEESE LOG

½ cup dried apricots	1 teaspoon poppy seeds
1 pound Monterey Jack (or mild Cheddar) cheese, shredded	½ teaspoon seasoned salt
	⅓ cup golden raisins
	⅓ cup chopped dates
1 package (8 ounces) cream cheese, softened	Chopped walnuts
	2 tablespoons chopped red candied cherries
⅓ cup dry sherry	

Soak the apricots in 1 cup of water for 2 hours, then drain, chop, and set aside. Blend the cheeses and add the sherry, poppy seeds and seasoned salt and mix well. Add the apricots, raisins and dates and mix thoroughly.

Turn out onto a sheet of foil and shape into a 9-inch log. Wrap securely in foil and chill until firm. Roll in the chopped nuts and candied cherries to coat, then cover again with foil and store in refrigerator until ready to give. *Makes one 2-pound log.*

GINGER-FILBERT CHEESE SPREAD

1 package (8 ounces) cream cheese or Neufchâtel cheese, softened	¼ cup minced preserved stem ginger
¼ cup finely chopped roasted filberts	1 tablespoon lemon juice

Mix together the cream cheese, filberts, ginger and lemon juice. Pack into a gift jar and store in the refrigerator to blend flavors until ready to give. Suggest serving at room temperature with crackers or buttered toast. *Makes about 1 cup.*

HICKORY-FLAVORED CHEESE SPREAD

1 package (8 ounces) cream cheese, softened	½ teaspoon hickory salt
1 cup finely shredded sharp Cheddar cheese	⅓ cup finely chopped toasted blanched almonds

With a wooden spoon, beat the cream cheese until fluffy; add Cheddar cheese and salt and continue to cream until well blended. Add almonds and mix well.

Pack into small crocks, cover and refrigerate until ready to give. Suggest serving at room temperature. *Makes about 1½ cups.*

LIPTAUER

This Austrian cheese spread is very perishable, so keep it refrigerated for no more than a day before giving.

1 tablespoon instant minced onion	1 teaspoon capers, finely minced
2 teaspoons dry mustard	1 tablespoon caraway seeds
½ cup butter or margarine, softened	Dash of ground white pepper
1 package (8 ounces) cream cheese, softened	Parsley flakes
2 anchovy fillets, finely minced	Paprika

Mix onion and mustard with 2 tablespoons of warm water and let stand 10 minutes. Cream the butter in a small mixer bowl. Gradually add the cream cheese, blending well. Add the onion-mustard mixture and the anchovies, capers, caraway seeds and pepper. Mix thoroughly and pack into a 2-cup bowl or glass. Chill until firm. Sprinkle with parsley and paprika before giving and suggest serving with crackers or crisp bread. *Makes about 2 cups.*

WISCONSIN CHEESE ROLL

¼ pound Cheddar cheese
½ cup unblanched almonds
2 packages (3 ounces each)
   cream cheese

1 tablespoon minced
   pimiento
Garlic salt
Paprika

Force the Cheddar cheese and almonds through a food chopper. Add the cream cheese and the pimiento. Season to taste with garlic salt and shape into a 1½-inch-wide roll. Sprinkle a piece of waxed paper with a thick layer of paprika; coat the cheese with the paprika and roll up in the paper. Store in the refrigerator until ready to give. *Makes one ½-pound roll.*

CHEESE ROUNDS

½ cup butter
1 cup grated sharp Cheddar
   cheese

1 cup unsifted flour
Pinch salt
Pinch cayenne

Preheat the oven to 375° F.
   Cream the butter and cheese well. Stir in the flour, salt and cayenne. Roll into ¾-inch balls. Bake 10 to 15 minutes. Cool, store in a cool place, or freeze. *Makes about 2 dozen.*

CHEESE TWISTS

1 box piecrust mix   Paprika
1 cup grated sharp Cheddar
  cheese

Preheat the oven to 450° F.
Pour piecrust mix into a medium-sized bowl. Add the grated cheese. Add liquid as indicated on the directions for the mix; blend ingredients. Roll out to ⅛-inch thickness, and cut into strips about ½ by 3 inches. Twist each strip several times and put on a cookie sheet. Sprinkle with paprika. Bake for 10 minutes. *Makes 48.*

These twists can be frozen until ready to give. Package them for giving in plastic bags tied with ribbon or standing upright in a small cup or mug wrapped in tissue paper.

CHICKEN-LIVER PÂTÉ

1 pound chicken livers   1 tablespoon Worcestershire
1 small onion, halved   ¼ teaspoon pepper
¾ cup chicken stock   ¾ cup butter
½ teaspoon paprika   Canned beef consommé
½ teaspoon curry powder   (gelatin type)
1 teaspoon salt

Simmer the chicken livers and the onion in the stock until done, about 5 minutes. Pour it all into a blender and add the paprika, curry powder, salt, Worcestershire and pepper. Blend until smooth. Add the butter, a little at a time, blending until smooth.

Put into gift containers and chill until set. When set, pour a thin layer of consommé over top. Keep refrigerated until ready to give. *Makes 3 cups.*

AVOCADO-TUNA DIP

1 medium avocado, peeled, pitted and cut into chunks
1 can (6½ to 7 ounces) tuna, drained
½ cup creamed cottage cheese
2 tablespoons lemon juice
Salt and pepper to taste

Beat the avocado, tuna, cottage cheese, lemon juice, salt and pepper with an electric beater until well blended but with some texture of the tuna remaining.

Pack into gift containers and keep refrigerated until ready to give. Give with instructions to serve as a dip with raw vegetables or crackers. *Makes 2 cups.*

TUNA SPREAD

2 cans (6½ or 7 ounces) chunk tuna, drained
6 ounces softened cream cheese
½ cup mayonnaise
1 small onion, sliced
½ teaspoon coarsely ground black pepper
¼ teaspoon hot pepper sauce
½ pound mushrooms, minced
Butter
3 tablespoons chopped parsley or dried parsley flakes
Stuffed green olives (optional)

Mix in an electric blender in the order given, or beat about 10 minutes with an electric beater, the tuna, cream cheese, mayonnaise, onion, pepper and hot sauce. Sauté the mushrooms in a

little butter until browned. Add the mushrooms and parsley to the tuna mixture. Stir and refrigerate. *Makes about 2½ cups.*
This spread will keep for several days in the refrigerator. Give it garnished with stuffed green olives, if you wish.

RATATOUILLE PROVENÇALE

1 medium eggplant, diced	2 medium onions, sliced
¾ cup olive oil	1 clove garlic, crushed
1 can (1 pound) plum tomatoes	2 tablespoons chopped parsley
1 jar (4 ounces) pimientos, drained	1 teaspoon capers
	Salt and pepper to taste

Sauté the eggplant in the oil in a heavy kettle for a few minutes. Add the tomatoes, pimientos, onions, garlic, parsley, capers, salt and pepper and cook slowly, stirring occasionally, for 20 minutes, or until mixture is thick. *Makes about 4 cups.*
Pack into a gift container and keep refrigerated until ready to give. It may be reheated before serving or served cold.

SPICED ALMONDS

1½ cups sifted confectioners' sugar	½ teaspoon chili powder
3 tablespoons cornstarch	1 teaspoon salt
2 teaspoons cinnamon	2 egg whites
½ teaspoon ground cloves	2 cups blanched whole almonds
½ teaspoon allspice	

Preheat the oven to 250° F.
Mix the sugar, cornstarch, cinnamon, cloves, allspice, chili powder and salt. Spread half the mixture on the bottom of a 10½ by 15½ by 1-inch jelly-roll pan. Beat the egg whites with

2 tablespoons of water. Dip the almonds in the egg white mixture, spread them on the sugar mixture in the pan, then sprinkle them with the remaining sugar mixture. Mix well to coat. Bake, stirring occasionally, for 1½ hours. Cool. Store in an airtight container until ready to give.

TERIYAKI ALMONDS

4 cups blanched almonds (1¼ pounds)	2 tablespoons soy sauce
	2 tablespoons sherry
	¼ to ½ teaspoon ground
¼ cup butter or margarine	ginger
	Garlic salt

Preheat the oven to 300° F.

Put the almonds in a 13 by 9 by 2-inch pan and toast in the oven 20 minutes. Meanwhile, melt the butter in a small saucepan. Add soy sauce, sherry and ginger and stir to blend. Pour over the almonds and toast, stirring occasionally to get an even coating, 15 to 20 minutes longer. Sprinkle with garlic salt to taste and spread out on a paper towel to dry and cool. Store in a cool place or freeze until ready to give. *Makes 4 cups.*

CURRIED CASHEWS

¼ cup butter	Salt
2 cups cashew nuts	
2 to 3 tablespoons curry powder	

Melt the butter in a skillet. Add the nuts and brown lightly, stirring frequently. Drain on paper towels. Sprinkle with the curry powder and salt to taste. Store in a cool place or freeze until ready to give. *Makes 2 cups.*

TOASTED PECANS

4 cups pecan halves (1¼ pounds)
¼ cup butter or margarine

1 teaspoon (or more) Angostura bitters
Seasoned salt

Preheat the oven to 300° F.

Put the pecans in a 13 by 9 by 2-inch pan and toast in the oven 20 minutes. Meanwhile, melt the butter in a small saucepan. Add bitters and 1 teaspoon seasoned salt and stir to blend. Pour over the pecans and toast, stirring occasionally to get an even coating, 15 minutes longer. Sprinkle with additional seasoned salt, if desired. Spread out on a paper towel to dry and cool. Store in a cool place or freeze. *Makes 4 cups.*

DILLED OLIVES

1 clove garlic, crushed
½ teaspoon dillweed

1 jar (9 ounces) large pimiento-stuffed olives

Add the garlic and dillweed to the liquid in the olive jar. Shake well. Store in the refrigerator at least several days to thoroughly season the olives. Give in a decorated glass jar.

OLIVE SURPRISES

¼ cup soft butter or margarine
1 cup grated sharp Cheddar cheese
¼ teaspoon each salt and paprika

½ cup sifted flour
3 dozen medium stuffed olives

Cream the butter and cheese until blended. Add the salt, paprika and flour and mix well. Chill 15 to 20 minutes.

Preheat the oven to 400° F. Shape a small portion of dough around each olive. Bake about 15 minutes. Refrigerate in a glass jar, ready to give, or freeze. Suggest serving hot or cold. *Makes 36.*

TOASTED COCONUT CHIPS

1 coconut   Salt to taste

Preheat the oven to 300° F.

To prepare coconut, pierce eyes in the end of the coconut and drain liquid. Roast coconut in a shallow pan in the oven 20 to 30 minutes, or until shell cracks in several places. Remove from oven and pound with hammer to crack coconut open. Remove meat in fairly large chunks when possible and run potato peeler down edges to make strips.

Spread half in roasting pan; sprinkle with salt and toast in 300° oven 20 to 25 minutes, stirring occasionally. Repeat with second batch. Cool.

Pack loosely in airtight decorated coffee cans topped with bows or in interesting jars. *Makes about 2 quarts.*

SEASONED SUNFLOWER OR PUMPKIN SEEDS

½ pound (about 1¾ cups)   1 tablespoon vegetable oil
    sunflower or pumpkin   2 teaspoons seasoned salt
    seeds   or garlic salt

Preheat the oven to 300° F.

Spread the seeds in a shallow pan and toast in the oven for 10 minutes. Drizzle with the oil, then sprinkle with the salt.

Mix well and toast, stirring often, 30 minutes longer. Add more salt, if you wish. Store in a covered container until ready to give.

Seasonings

GIVE ONE OR MORE of these specially seasoned butters, herb mixtures, sauces or vinegars to friends who like to cook. They will enjoy experimenting with new flavorings and will be delighted with your ingenuity.

Ideas for Giving Seasonings

Seasoned butters can be packed in disposable plastic glasses, margarine tubs with lids, crocks, small soufflé dishes or custard cups. Keep them refrigerated, and give them only when you do not have very far to travel. Add a loaf of homemade bread (pp. 45–65) to the gift, if you wish, or some Brioches (p. 58) or Croissants (p. 62).

Give herb mixtures in small spice jars or use one to fill a new bulb-type meat baster with the opening taped over so that the herbs don't spill out. You can wrap mixed herbs in a plastic bag, tie it with a bow and present it in a mortar with a pestle or in a tiny basket with a handle.

Give mustard in a mustard pot, together with a little spoon. Put sauces and dressings in ceramic bottles, vinegars in clear glass ones that display their lovely colors. Save nicely shaped long, skinny bottles or buy new glass bottles or cruets, which are available in a handsome array. Tie a new basting brush to the bottle, if you wish.

All seasonings should be labeled. Wherever possible, give

the ingredients and suggest ways in which the seasoning should be used.

HONEY BUTTER

½ cup honey
1 cup softened butter or
  margarine

½ cup chopped walnuts

Gradually beat the honey into the butter until fluffy. Stir in the nuts. Pack into gift containers and store tightly covered in the refrigerator until ready to give. Suggest softening it slightly at room temperature before serving with toast, crackers or biscuits. Can be used as seasoning in cooking. *Makes about 2 cups.*

ONION-MUSTARD BUTTER

1 cup softened butter or
  margarine
⅓ cup finely chopped green
  onion

1 tablespoon prepared
  mustard

Combine the butter with the onion and the mustard. Pack into a gift container and store tightly covered in the refrigerator until ready to give. Suggest softening at room temperature before serving with rolls or dark bread, or using as seasoning in cooking. *Makes 1½ cups.*

SAVORY BUTTER

1 tablespoon instant minced
   onion
2 teaspoons lemon juice
½ pound softened butter or
   margarine

2 tablespoons parsley flakes
¼ teaspoon ground marjoram
¼ teaspoon ground thyme
   Pinch of garlic powder

Soak the onion in the lemon juice for 10 minutes to rehydrate. Put the butter in a bowl and add the onion, parsley flakes, marjoram, thyme and garlic powder. Mix thoroughly, pack into a gift container and refrigerate until ready to give. Suggest using it to season vegetables or popcorn or to spread on bread before toasting it in the oven. *Makes 1 cup.*

SHRIMP BUTTER

¼ pound softened butter or
   margarine
1 can (4½ ounces) shrimps,
   drained and chopped

¼ teaspoon dillweed
2 teaspoons lemon juice
   Freshly ground pepper to
   taste

Blend the butter, shrimp, dillweed, lemon juice and pepper together very well. Pack into a gift container and store in the refrigerator until ready to give. Suggest softening at room temperature before serving with crackers or bread. Can be used to season rice. *Makes 1 cup.*

HERB BUTTER

½ pound softened butter
  or margarine
3 to 4 tablespoons finely
  chopped fresh herbs:
  parsley, tarragon,
  marjoram, basil,
  thyme

1 teaspoon salt
Pepper
Lemon juice

Cream the butter and beat in any fresh herb or herb mixture available. Season with the salt and with pepper and lemon juice to taste. Pack into a gift container and refrigerate until ready to give. Suggest using as a seasoning for noodles, potatoes, vegetables, meat, or just about anything else. *Makes 1 cup.*

MILD CURRY POWDER

Use a mortar and pestle or a blender to crush the coriander, fennel and fenugreek.

3 tablespoons plus 2
  teaspoons crushed
  coriander seed
1 teaspoon crushed fennel
1 tablespoon plus 2
  teaspoons crushed
  fenugreek
1 tablespoon plus 2
  teaspoons cumin

2½ teaspoons white pepper
5 tablespoons turmeric
½ teaspoon cayenne
2 tablespoons ground car-
  damom
1 teaspoon ground cloves

Mix all ingredients together thoroughly. Wrap in a plastic bag until ready to package and give. *Makes 1 cup.*

HOT CURRY POWDER

*Use a mortar and pestle or a blender to crush the coriander,
fennel and fenugreek.*

4 tablespoons crushed
coriander seed
1 teaspoon crushed fennel
1 tablespoon plus 2
teaspoons crushed
fenugreek
1 tablespoon plus 2
teaspoons cumin

2½ teaspoons finely ground
black pepper
3 tablespoons turmeric
1 tablespoon cayenne
2 tablespoons ground
cardamom
1 teaspoon ground cloves
1 tablespoon ground ginger

Mix all ingredients together thoroughly. Wrap in a plastic bag
until ready to package and give. *Makes 1 cup.*

HERB SALT

¼ cup coarse salt
2 teaspoons coarsely ground
pepper
1 teaspoon whole oregano,
crushed
2 bay leaves, finely crushed
1 teaspoon rosemary leaves,
crushed

½ teaspoon onion powder
1 teaspoon celery seed
2 teaspoons thyme leaves,
crushed
1 teaspoon marjoram leaves,
crushed

Mix all ingredients thoroughly. Wrap in a plastic bag until
ready to package and give. Suggest using as a dip for raw vegetables or as seasoning for cooked vegetables. *Makes ¼ cup.*

ONION-RICE MIX

2 cups uncooked rice
1 envelope (1¾ ounces)
  onion soup mix

1 teaspoon parsley flakes
½ teaspoon salt

Mix together the rice, onion soup mix, parsley flakes and salt and combine thoroughly. Divide in half and package each half in a plastic bag tied with a ribbon, or in a small jar. *Each package will make 4 to 6 servings.*

Give each with the following cooking instructions: "Combine the onion-rice mix with 2 cups of cold water and 1 tablespoon of butter or margarine in a heavy saucepan. Bring to a boil over high heat, then cover tightly and cook over very low heat for 15 minutes, or until the liquid is absorbed."

LEMON-DILL RICE MIX

2 cups uncooked rice
3 teaspoons bottled dried
  grated lemon peel
2 teaspoons dillweed
1 teaspoon dried minced
  chives

1 teaspoon salt
4 teaspoons chicken stock
  base or bouillon
  powder

Mix together the rice, lemon peel, dillweed, chives, salt and chicken stock base and combine thoroughly. Divide in half and package each half in a plastic bag tied with a ribbon, or in a small jar. *Each package will make 4 to 6 servings.*

Give each with the following cooking instructions: "Combine the lemon-dill rice mix with 2 cups of cold water and 1 tablespoon of butter or margarine in a heavy saucepan. Bring to a boil over high heat, then cover tightly and cook over very low heat for 15 minutes, or until the liquid is absorbed."

BARBADOS BARBECUE SAUCE

½ cup unsulfured molasses
⅓ cup prepared yellow
    mustard
½ cup cider vinegar

2 tablespoons Worcester-
    shire sauce
½ teaspoon hot pepper sauce
1 cup catsup

Combine all ingredients thoroughly. Put in a container with a tight-fitting lid and store in the refrigerator or a cool place until ready to give. *Makes 2⅓ cups.*

TEXAS HOT BARBECUE SAUCE

2 cups catsup
⅔ cup Worcestershire sauce
½ cup vinegar
1 teaspoon salt

2 cloves garlic, minced
Dash of cayenne
2 tablespoons vegetable oil

In a saucepan, mix the catsup, Worcestershire sauce, vinegar, salt, garlic, cayenne and oil. Bring to a boil, then simmer for 20 minutes. Pour into hot, sterilized, ½-pint jars and seal. *Makes 2½ pints.*

FRENCH DRESSING

2 tablespoons lemon juice
2 tablespoons vinegar
¾ cup olive or salad oil
1 teaspoon seasoned salt
¼ teaspoon pepper

½ teaspoon steak sauce
½ teaspoon paprika
¼ teaspoon garlic powder
½ teaspoon sugar

Mix all ingredients thoroughly—either in a blender, with a rotary beater, or by shaking in a jar. *Makes 1 cup.*

GREEN GODDESS DRESSING

1½ cups mayonnaise
⅔ cup sour cream
3 tablespoons vinegar
2 tablespoons lemon
   juice
2 small cloves garlic,
   minced

⅓ cup chives, finely
   chopped
½ cup parsley, finely
   chopped
4 to 5 flat anchovies, minced
   Salt and freshly ground
   pepper

Combine all the ingredients thoroughly. *Makes about 3 cups.*
Pack in gift jars and keep refrigerated until ready to give.
Suggest that it be used cold with salads and seafood.

MUSTARDY SALAD DRESSING

¼ cup sugar
2 teaspoons salt
3 tablespoons flour
2 eggs
1½ cups milk

Mild yellow prepared
   mustard
2 tablespoons butter or
   margarine
½ cup cider vinegar

Mix the sugar, salt, flour, eggs, milk and 2 teaspoons of mustard in the top of a double boiler. Beat with a rotary beater
until well blended. Add the butter and cook over hot water,
stirring, until thick. Remove from the heat and stir in the
vinegar. Cool, then blend in ¼ cup of mustard. *Makes about
2 cups.*

Put the dressing in a pretty jar and keep refrigerated until
ready to give. Suggest using it on egg or potato salad.

POPPY-SEED FRUIT DRESSING

⅓ cup sugar
1 teaspoon dry mustard
1 teaspoon salt

⅓ cup white vinegar
1 cup salad oil
2 tablespoons poppy seeds

Mix the sugar, mustard, salt and vinegar in a small bowl. Add the oil, a little at a time, beating well after each addition. Stir in the poppy seeds. *Makes 1½ cups.*

Give in a pretty jar with a note saying that it is especially good on fruit salad.

ROQUEFORT DRESSING

½ pound Roquefort (or
  blue) cheese
1 teaspoon dried onion flakes
1 teaspoon sugar
1 teaspoon paprika
¼ teaspoon pepper

½ teaspoon dry mustard
1 teaspoon Worcestershire
  sauce
⅔ cup cider vinegar
2 cups salad oil

Crumble the cheese into a large bowl and add the onion flakes, sugar, paprika, pepper, dry mustard, Worcestershire sauce and vinegar. Beat until fairly smooth. Gradually add the oil, beating until smooth. Put in pretty jars and keep refrigerated until ready to give. *Makes 3 cups.*

SHARP LEMON SAUCE

¾ cup grated lemon rind
   (about 12 lemons)
3 cups lemon juice (about
   12 lemons)
¼ cup mustard seed
1 tablespoon each turmeric
   and white pepper

1 teaspoon each whole cloves
   and mace
2 tablespoons each sugar and
   salt

Mix all ingredients together in a saucepan and let stand 1½ hours. Bring to a boil, then simmer gently, stirring occasionally, for 30 minutes. Pour into a glass casserole with a cover and let stand 2 weeks, stirring every day, if possible.

After 2 weeks, mix well by shaking, or put in a blender. Pour into sterilized bottles and seal until ready to give. Suggest using as a condiment with meat or fish. *Makes about four ½-pints.*

EXTRA-HOT MUSTARD

½ cup dry mustard
1 tablespoon flour
2 tablespoons cider vinegar

1 tablespoon brandy
3 tablespoons sugar

Combine the mustard and flour in a small mixing bowl. Gradually stir in ¼ cup of boiling water. Let stand, stirring occasionally, for 30 minutes.

Add the vinegar, brandy and sugar and mix well. Put in a small jar and store at least a week before giving. *Makes ½ cup.*

SAVORY MUSTARD SAUCE

2 tablespoons Dijon-style
   mustard
2 tablespoons wine vinegar
½ cup oil
1 tablespoon sugar

1 teaspoon dried dillweed, or
   to taste
¼ teaspoon salt
⅛ teaspoon pepper

Using a fork, beat the mustard and vinegar together in a small bowl until well blended and smooth. Gradually beat in the oil until the sauce is smooth, shiny and thick. Stir in the sugar, dillweed, salt and pepper. You can also make this in a blender.

Store in a jar in a cool place until ready to give. Suggest serving this sauce with seafood. *Makes about ¾ cup.*

SHERRY PEPPERS

Small, hot red or green
   peppers

½ to 1 cup medium-dry
   sherry

Slit the peppers lengthwise. Pack them without crushing in a small jug or bottle. Pour the sherry over them. Close tightly with a cork or screw top and let stand 4 or 5 days before giving. Suggest sprinkling the spicy liquid lightly to season cooked greens, salads, soups, stews and curries. *Makes ½ to 1 cup.*

CEYLON SPICED TEA

12 cardamom pods
1½ teaspoons cracked
      cinnamon
1 tablespoon bottled dry
      grated orange peel

8 whole cloves, crushed
½ cup loose tea

Open the cardamom pods, remove the seeds and crush them slightly. Mix them with the cinnamon, orange peel, cloves and tea. Pack in a pretty jar and give with instructions to use 1 rounded teaspoon for each cup of tea and to brew it for 5 or 6 minutes.

FRUITED WINE VINEGAR

1½ cups white-wine vinegar
½ cup white table grapes
2 pieces fresh pineapple,
      cut in sticks

Twist of orange rind
1 strip pickled red pepper

Warm the vinegar in a saucepan. Place the grapes, pineapple, orange rind and pepper in a sterilized jar or bottle and pour in the warmed vinegar. Cap and allow to stand for a few days before giving. *Makes 1 pint.*

SPICED VINEGAR

1 pint red-wine vinegar
1 bay leaf
1 teaspoon whole allspice
1 teaspoon coriander seeds
1 teaspoon shelled cardamom
    seeds

1 stick cinnamon
6 whole cloves
2 tablespoons sugar

Combine all ingredients in the top part of a double boiler. Over boiling water, heat mixture until simmering. Turn off heat, cover and steep 2 hours.

Leave the spices in the vinegar and pour into clean glass bottles with stoppers. Store in a cool place until ready to give. *Makes about 2 cups.*

HERB VINEGAR

2 or 3 long sprigs of fresh
    tarragon, rosemary, dill,
    thyme, marjoram or
    oregano

1 pint white wine or cider
    vinegar

Put the herb sprigs of your choice in a pretty glass bottle. Pour the vinegar over them and let stand in a cool place for 2 or 3 weeks before giving. *Makes 2 cups.*

Breads and Rolls

BAKING BREAD is an immensely satisfying experience. Every stage in the process has its own special pleasure—kneading the dough to a smooth, satiny mass, checking as the dough rises, and the rich and wonderful smell of bread baking in the oven. All of these contribute to that unique feeling of satisfaction and accomplishment that every bread-baker knows.

Home-baked bread is not only a pleasure to make; it is also a wonderful present to give. A beautiful, crusty loaf has an old-fashioned wholesomeness that is particularly welcome today when most commercial breads are full of preservatives and have an artificial, unappealing texture. Homemade bread is appropriate for just about any occasion. These recipes offer a variety of yeast and baking power breads and rolls from which to choose.

Some of these gift breads should be made no more than a day or two ahead so that they will be fresh when presented. Others will keep for about a week, well wrapped, in a breadbox or in the refrigerator. Breads take well to freezing: make a few when you're in the mood, freeze them and you will have a supply on hand for instant gift-giving.

Tips on Baking Bread

• Compressed yeast is interchangeable with dry yeast, though compressed yeast requires lukewarm water (80° to 95° F.) for dissolving. These recipes specify dry yeast only because it is more readily available and keeps longer.

• Be sure to dissolve dry yeast in water that is just the right temperature. It should be quite warm: 105° to 115° F.

• To knead, flour your hands and the board lightly, shape the dough into a ball, fold it toward you and then push it away from you with the heels of your hands; give the dough a quarter-turn and repeat the action until the dough is smooth and elastic.

• If you have one, you can use the dough hook attachment to an electric mixer instead of kneading by hand.

• Let the dough rise in a warm, draft-free place (75° to 85° F.). If the room is too cold, set the bowl in an unheated oven or on a rack placed over a bowl of hot water.

• Test dough by pressing two fingers ½ inch into it; if the indentation remains, the dough has fully risen.

• Brush bread with melted butter during baking for a soft crust. Sprinkle it with water during baking for a crisp crust.

• When bread is done, it will pull away from the sides of the pan and will sound hollow when you tap the bottom and sides of the loaf.

• Let bread cool on a rack. Cover it with a towel while it is cooling, if you want a soft crust; leave it uncovered for a crisp one.

• Cool bread completely before wrapping it.

• Bread freezes well. Make sure it is well wrapped in foil. Allow about 3 hours for it to defrost at room temperature, or put it, still wrapped and frozen, in a preheated 300° to 350° F. oven until heated through—about 30 minutes. Bread should be eaten soon after defrosting since breads that have been frozen dry out more quickly than fresh ones.

Ideas for Giving Bread

If you wish to embellish your gift of bread, buy an attractive bread board and wrap the bread on the board, using bright yellow tissue paper or cellophane, tied with an orange yarn bow.

A small crock of your own Herb Butter (p. 34) or a jar of home-made jam or jelly (pp. 171–82) goes well with most breads. Other gift companions might be a good serrated bread knife, a pretty butter spreader, or a large ceramic mixing bowl. You can also wrap bread in a new, teflon-lined bread pan or in a pretty and useful breadbox.

If the bread you are giving has a special ingredient that might be hard to find, such as rye flour, stone-ground cornmeal, candied fruit or poppy seeds, put the proper amount in a can-nister or glass jar and give it and the bread recipe along with the bread.

Wrap rolls in a pretty basket lined with a crisp, blue-and-white-checked napkin.

Decorate sweet Christmas breads with candied green pine-apple and red cherries, and wrap them in red or gold foil. Give them on a wooden tray adorned with evergreen branches and red berries.

APPLESAUCE-PECAN BREAD

2 large eggs
1 cup canned applesauce
1 cup granulated sugar
⅓ cup vegetable oil
3 tablespoons milk
1 teaspoon cinnamon
¼ teaspoon nutmeg
1 teaspoon baking soda
½ teaspoon baking powder

½ teaspoon salt
2 cups all-purpose flour
1¼ cups finely chopped
    pecans
½ cup mixed candied fruit
¼ cup packed light brown
    sugar
Confectioners' sugar
    (optional)

Preheat the oven to 350° F.

In a large bowl, beat the eggs until foamy. Stir in the apple-sauce, sugar, oil and milk. In a separate bowl, mix ½ teaspoon of the cinnamon with the nutmeg, baking soda, baking powder, salt and flour; gradually add this mixture to the first mixture, beating with a spoon until it is well mixed. Stir in 1 cup of the nuts and the fruit. Spread in a well-greased 9 by 5 by 3-inch loaf pan.

Mix the remaining cinnamon and nuts with the brown sugar. Sprinkle evenly on top of the batter and press lightly with your hand. Bake for 1 hour or until done, spreading a piece of foil over the bread during the last half hour of baking so that it does not get too brown. Cool on a rack. Sprinkle with confectioners' sugar, if you wish. *Makes one 9-inch loaf.*

Wrapped in foil and stored in the refrigerator, this bread will keep for about a week. It can also be frozen.

BANANA BREAD

1 egg	1 teaspoon baking soda
1 cup sugar	½ cup chopped dates
½ cup shortening	½ cup chopped maraschino
3 ripe bananas, mashed	cherries (red and
1 teaspoon vanilla extract	green)
2 cups all-purpose flour	½ cup chopped nuts

Preheat the oven to 350° F.

Beat the egg, sugar, shortening, bananas and vanilla together in a large bowl until smooth. Sift the flour and baking soda together and blend into the banana mixture. Stir in the dates, cherries and nuts.

Pour the batter into a greased and floured 9 by 5 by 3-inch pan or into one fluted tube pan (4-cup capacity) and one small loaf pan. Bake for 1 hour and 15 minutes, or until done. The time will vary according to the size and shape of the pans. *Makes one 9-inch loaf or one small ring and one small loaf.*

Wrapped in foil and refrigerated, this bread will keep for about a week. It can also be frozen.

CHALLAH

This is the braided bread traditionally served on Jewish holidays or the Sabbath.

1 envelope active dry yeast	2 eggs
2 tablespoons sugar	2 tablespoons oil
1½ cups warm water	1 egg yolk, slightly beaten
About 5 cups flour	2 tablespoons poppy seeds
2 teaspoons salt	

Preheat the oven to 375° F.

Combine the yeast, sugar and ¼ cup warm water. Let stand 5 minutes. Sift 4½ cups of flour and the salt into a large bowl. Make a well in the center and drop in the eggs, oil, remaining 1¼ cups of warm water and the yeast mixture. Work liquids into flour. Knead on floured board until dough is smooth and elastic, kneading in enough more flour to make a manageable dough. Place in a bowl, brush the top with oil, cover with a towel and let stand in a warm place to rise 1 hour. Punch down, cover and let rise until doubled in bulk.

Divide dough into 3 equal parts. Between lightly floured hands roll dough into 3 strips of even length. Braid these and place on a greased cookie sheet. Cover and let rise until doubled. Brush with the egg yolk and sprinkle with the poppy seeds. Bake in the oven 45 to 50 minutes, or until golden brown.

This recipe makes 1 very large loaf or 2 smaller loaves. It can be used for a pan loaf or for rolls instead of for braided bread.

CINNAMON LOAF

1 package active dry yeast	Margarine
3 cups all-purpose flour	⅔ cup milk
½ cup granulated sugar	2 eggs, slightly beaten
½ teaspoon salt	1½ teaspoons cinnamon

In the large bowl of an electric mixer, combine the undissolved yeast with 1 cup of flour, ¼ cup granulated sugar and the salt and mix thoroughly. Heat ¼ cup margarine with the milk over low heat until warm (margarine need not melt). Add to dry ingredients. Beat at medium speed, scraping bowl occasionally, for 2 minutes. Add ½ cup flour, or enough to make a thick batter. Add eggs and beat at high speed, scraping bowl occasionally, for 2 minutes. Stir in remaining flour.

Turn dough out on a lightly floured board and knead until smooth and elastic. Put in a greased bowl, and cover and let rise in a warm place free from drafts for 1 hour, or until doubled in bulk. Punch down and knead lightly. Roll out on lightly floured board to an 18 by 9-inch rectangle. Spread with ¼ cup margarine, softened, and sprinkle with combined remaining sugar and the cinnamon. Roll up tightly, starting from narrow end, and put, seam side down, in a greased 9 by 5 by 3-inch loaf pan. Let rise 45 minutes, or until doubled.

Preheat the oven to 325° F.

With scissors dipped in flour, make a deep cut across loaf about 1 inch from end. Fold back toward one corner. Repeat down entire loaf, leaving about 1 inch between cuts and at other end and folding dough back alternately to opposite corners. Bake 45 minutes, or until done. Brush with melted margarine. Cool about 10 minutes in pan, loosen with spatula and turn out on rack to cool. *Makes one 9-inch loaf.*

CRANBERRY-ORANGE TEA BREAD

2 cups all-purpose flour	2 cups fresh cranberries,
1½ teaspoons baking powder	coarsely chopped
½ teaspoon baking soda	Grated rind and juice of
½ teaspoon salt	1 orange
1 cup sugar	¼ cup margarine, melted
½ cup finely chopped	1 egg, well beaten
walnuts	

Preheat the oven to 350° F.

Combine well in a mixing bowl the flour, baking powder, baking soda, salt, sugar, walnuts and cranberries. Combine the orange rind, juice and margarine with enough water to make ¾ cup. Beat in the egg. Pour the liquid mixture over the dry ingredients and mix just enough to dampen.

Spoon into a greased 9 by 5 by 3-inch loaf pan and bake for 1 hour and 10 minutes, or until done. Turn out and cool on a rack. *Makes one 9-inch loaf.*

Well-wrapped and stored in an airtight container, this bread will keep about a week.

CRANBERRY WHOLE-WHEAT BREAD

9 cups whole-wheat flour
1 package active dry yeast
2 tablespoons butter or
    margarine
3 tablespoons honey
½ cup sugar
2 teaspoons salt

¼ cup nonfat dry-milk
    granules
¾ cup chopped nuts
2 cups fresh or frozen
    cranberries, coarsely
    chopped

Mix 3 cups of flour with the yeast in the large bowl of an electric mixer. Put 3 cups of water in a saucepan over low heat, add the butter, honey, sugar, salt and dry milk and heat until very warm (120° to 130° F.) Pour over flour mixture and beat at medium speed, scraping bowl occasionally, for 3 minutes. Stir in the remaining flour and the nuts and berries.

Turn out on a floured board and knead 8 to 10 minutes. Put in a greased bowl and turn to grease the top. Let rise in a warm place 1¼ hours, or until doubled in bulk. Punch down and divide in half. Roll each half into a 14 by 9-inch rectangle. Roll up, starting at the short end, and shape in a loaf. Seal ends and put in 2 greased 9 by 5 by 3-inch loaf pans. Cover and let rise in a warm place 1 hour, or until doubled in bulk. Bake in a preheated 375° F. oven for 45 to 50 minutes. Cool on a wire rack. *Makes two 9-inch loaves.*

FINNISH-STYLE HEALTH BREAD

1 envelope active dry yeast	1¼ cups whole-rye flour
¼ cup warm water	1¼ cups whole-wheat flour
2¼ cups buttermilk	Wheat germ
1 teaspoon salt	2 cups all-purpose flour

Dissolve the yeast in the ¼ cup of warm water (105° to 115° F.) in a mixing bowl. Add the buttermilk, salt, and rye and wheat flours together with ¼ cup wheat germ, and stir with a wooden spoon until well blended. Gradually add the all-purpose flour, beating until smooth. Turn out on a floured board and beat until smooth and elastic. Cover loosely and let rest on the board 30 minutes.

Divide the dough into 2 equal pieces and pat each into a round cake 6 inches in diameter. Brush with water and press the tops into some wheat germ. Put on a lightly greased baking sheet. Let rise 1 hour or until doubled in bulk. Cut a crisscross pattern on the tops with a very sharp knife. Bake in a preheated 400° F. oven for 30 minutes, or until done. Cool on rack. *Makes two 8-inch round loaves.*

FRENCH BREAD

1 package active dry yeast	1 tablespoon sugar
¼ cup warm water	¾ cup cold water
1 cup boiling water	6 cups flour
1 tablespoon shortening	1 egg white
2 teaspoons salt	

Sprinkle the yeast on the ¼ cup of warm water. Let stand a few minutes, then stir until dissolved. Pour 1 cup of boiling water over the shortening, salt and sugar in a large mixing bowl. Add ¾ cup of cold water and cool until lukewarm. Add the yeast mixture and gradually beat in enough flour to form a stiff dough. Turn out on a floured pastry cloth or board and knead until smooth and satiny. Put in a greased bowl, turn once, cover and let rise 1½ hours or until doubled.

Shape into 2 oblong loaves each about 14 inches long. Put on greased baking sheets. Let rise 1 hour or until doubled.

Preheat the oven to 425° F. Brush the loaves with beaten egg white and, with a knife, make 3 slashes across the tops. Bake 30 minutes; reduce heat to 350° F. and bake 20 minutes. *Makes two 14-inch loaves.*

FRUIT-NUT BREAD

1¾ cups all-purpose flour
1 cup sugar
½ teaspoon salt
4 teaspoons baking powder
1 cup coarsely chopped
    walnuts
½ cup mixed candied fruit

1 egg, well beaten
Grated rind of 1 lemon
    (1 tablespoon)
¾ cup evaporated milk
2 tablespoons butter or
    margarine, melted

Preheat the oven to 350° F.

Mix the flour, sugar, salt and baking powder in a medium bowl. Stir in the nuts and fruit. Mix the egg, grated lemon rind, milk and butter with ½ cup of water. Add to the first mixture and stir just until all the dry ingredients are moistened.

Bake in a well-greased 9 by 5 by 3-inch loaf pan for 60 to 65 minutes. Remove from the oven, let stand for 10 minutes, then turn out and cool on a rack. *Makes one 9-inch loaf.*

Wrapped in foil and stored in the refrigerator, this bread will keep for about a week. It can also be frozen.

OATMEAL BREAD

1 cup quick-cooking (not instant) rolled oats	½ cup molasses
2 cups milk, scalded	2 teaspoons salt
1 package active dry yeast	¼ teaspoon ground ginger
½ cup warm water	4½ cups all-purpose flour

Put the oats in a large bowl and cover with the milk. Stir and let stand until lukewarm. Sprinkle the yeast on the ½ cup of warm water. Let stand a few minutes, then stir until dissolved. Add the yeast mixture, molasses, salt and ginger to the oat mixture. Gradually stir in the 4½ cups of flour, mixing well. Cover and let rise in a warm place until doubled in bulk, about 1 hour.

Knead on a well-floured board and put into 2 greased 9 by 5 by 3-inch loaf pans. Let rise until almost doubled, about 45 minutes. Bake in a preheated 350° F. oven 45 to 50 minutes. *Makes two 9-inch loaves.*

SOUR RYE BREAD

This is a coarse bread with a fermented flavor. The dough should be mixed the night before baking and allowed to rise overnight.

2 envelopes active dry yeast	1 tablespoon salt
3½ cups warm water	1 tablespoon cumin seed, lightly crushed
8 cups whole-rye flour	3½ to 4 cups all-purpose flour
¼ cup molasses	

The night before you plan to bake the bread, sprinkle the yeast on top of the 3½ cups of warm water in a large mixing bowl;

stir to dissolve. Gradually stir in the rye flour. Cover the dough with a wet, clean towel to prevent a skin from forming and let it rise at room temperature overnight.

Early the next morning, punch the dough down; add the molasses, salt and cumin seed and about 1 cup of all-purpose flour and mix well. Gradually stir in more flour until a stiff dough is formed. Turn out on a floured board and knead until smooth and elastic. Divide into 3 equal pieces and shape each into a smooth loaf about 12 inches long. Put them on a large, greased baking sheet and let them rise in a warm, draft-free place for 35 to 40 minutes, or until a few cracks develop in the tops of the loaves.

While the dough is rising, preheat the oven to 350° F.

Bake for 1 hour, or until the bread is done, brushing once with hot water toward the end of the baking time. Brush again with hot water, then put on a rack to cool. This bread can be frozen. *Makes three 12-inch loaves.*

RYE AND WHOLE-WHEAT BREAD

2 cups milk
¼ cup sugar
¼ cup butter or margarine
3 tablespoons old-fashioned molasses
2 teaspoons salt
½ teaspoon baking soda
1 teaspoon grated orange rind and/or caraway seeds
1 package active dry yeast
3 cups (about) each rye and whole-wheat flours

Scald the milk and pour over next 5 ingredients in a large bowl. Add orange rind, if desired, and, if necessary, cool to luke-warm. Soften yeast in ½ cup warm water; stir until dissolved, then add to first mixture. Add rye flour and beat until smooth. Cover with a sheet of plastic wrap and let stand in a warm place for 30 minutes, or until bubbly. Stir in enough whole-wheat flour to make a firm dough. Turn out on a lightly floured board and knead 10 minutes, or until dough is smooth and no longer sticks to board. Put in a greased bowl and turn greased side up. Cover with a sheet of plastic wrap and let rise 1 hour, or until doubled.

Punch down and shape into 2 loaves. Put in 2 greased 9 by 5 by 3-inch loaf pans (or other pans), cover and let rise 45 minutes, or until light. Bake in a preheated 325° F. oven about 45 minutes. Turn out on a rack to cool. *Makes two 9-inch loaves.*

BRIOCHES

Brioche dough should be prepared the day before you plan to bake and allowed to rise for the second time overnight. These delightful little rolls are well worth the time involved in making them.

1 package active dry yeast	4 cups sifted flour
¼ cup warm water	3 eggs
¾ cup soft butter	5 egg yolks
¼ cup sugar	1 egg yolk beaten with 1
½ teaspoon salt	teaspoon milk
½ cup milk, scalded	(optional)

Soften the yeast in ¼ cup of warm water; let stand 5 minutes. Meanwhile, in a large bowl combine the soft butter, sugar, salt, and milk; cool to lukewarm; mix thoroughly. Add the yeast mixture and ½ cup of the flour; mix well. Add 1½ more cups of flour gradually, beating after each addition. Add the eggs and egg yolks one at a time, beating after each addition only enough to form a soft dough. Add the remaining 2 cups of flour, and beat about 5 minutes. Put in a large greased bowl; turn to bring greased side up. Cover with waxed paper and a towel, and let stand in a warm place (80° to 85° F.) 1½ hours, or until doubled in bulk. Punch down, cover, and set in the refrigerator for about 12 hours. Punch down dough occasionally as it rises.

To prepare for making, remove from refrigerator, punch down dough, turn out on a lightly floured board; let rest 10 minutes. Shape ⅔ of the dough into 18 2-inch balls. Put one in each cup of greased muffin pans; with your finger, make an impression in the top of each ball. Divide remaining ⅓ of dough into 18 small balls, and roll each into a cone shape between the palms of your hands. Insert tip of a cone in each impression in the large balls to make top hats. Cover with waxed paper and a towel; set in a warm place to double in bulk.

While the rolls are rising, preheat the oven to 425° F.

If you wish to glaze the rolls, brush the tops lightly with 1 egg yolk beaten slightly with 1 teaspoon of milk. Bake for 15 minutes, or until golden brown. Loosen with a spatula and lift gently out of pans. *Makes 1½ dozen brioches.*

Brioches freeze well. They should be heated before serving and served warm.

QUICK BUTTERMILK BUNS

½ cup butter or margarine,
    softened
About 1¼ cups sugar
1 egg
2½ cups flour, lightly
    spooned into cup

¼ teaspoon salt
½ teaspoon baking soda
½ teaspoon baking powder
1 cup buttermilk
Chopped nuts

Preheat the oven to 375° F.

Cream the butter, add ¾ cup sugar and cream until light and fluffy. Beat in the egg.

Sift the flour, salt, baking soda and baking powder. Add the buttermilk and the sifted dry ingredients alternately into the first mixture, mixing only until blended.

Drop by heaping tablespoonfuls on lightly greased baking sheets, 12 to a sheet. Sprinkle with nuts and sugar. Bake 15 minutes. *Makes 2 dozen.*

CINNAMON-RAISIN MUFFINS

1½ cups whole-wheat flour
⅓ cup packed brown sugar
3 teaspoons baking powder
½ teaspoon salt
1 teaspoon cinnamon
½ cup wheat germ

¾ cup unsulfured raisins
⅔ cup milk
⅓ cup soy or other cold-
    pressed oil
2 eggs, slightly beaten

Preheat the oven to 400° F.

In a large bowl, mix the flour, sugar, baking powder, salt, cinnamon, wheat germ and raisins. Add the milk, oil and eggs and mix only until dry ingredients are moistened. Fill greased 2½-inch muffin-pan sections ⅔ full and bake about 20 minutes. *Makes 1 dozen.*

BRAN-RAISIN BREAD

1 cup boiling water
1½ cups raisins
2 teaspoons baking soda
1½ cups flour
1 cup bran cereal, crushed

1 cup sugar
¼ teaspoon salt
1 egg
¼ cup oil

Preheat the oven to 350° F.

Pour the boiling water over the raisins and baking soda in a small mixing bowl; cool. In a larger bowl, stir together the flour, cereal, sugar and salt. Beat the egg and oil together lightly with a fork and stir into the dry mixture. Stir in the raisin mixture.

Spoon the mixture into 3 greased 1-pound cans, saved from canned fruits or vegetables. Bake for 45 minutes, or until a pick inserted in the center comes out clean. Cool in the cans on a rack for 10 minutes, then turn out onto the rack to cool completely. *Makes 3 loaves.*

The cans make good mailers for long-distance giving.

DOUBLE-CORN STICKS

1 cup sifted flour	¼ teaspoon baking soda
1 cup yellow cornmeal	2 tablespoons butter
2 tablespoons sugar	1 egg, slightly beaten
1½ teaspoons baking powder	¾ cup cream-style corn
1 teaspoon salt	⅔ cup buttermilk

Preheat the oven to 425° F.

Sift together the flour, cornmeal, sugar, baking powder, salt and baking soda in a large bowl. Cut in the butter. Add the egg, corn and buttermilk; mix just enough to dampen the dry ingredients.

Fill well-greased corn-stick pans or muffin pans ⅔ full. Bake about 20 minutes. *Makes about 1 dozen corn sticks.*

Corn sticks freeze well.

SESAME AND WHEAT-GERM CORN STICKS

¼ cup all-purpose flour	½ cup wheat germ
3 tablespoons sugar	¼ cup sesame seed
½ teaspoon salt	1 cup buttermilk
¾ teaspoon baking soda	⅓ cup vegetable oil
1 cup yellow cornmeal	1 egg

Preheat the oven to 350° F.

Mix the flour, sugar, salt and baking soda in a medium-sized bowl. Add the cornmeal, wheat germ and sesame seed and mix thoroughly. Combine the buttermilk and oil and blend in the egg. Add the liquid ingredients all at once to the dry ingredients and stir just until dry ingredients are moistened. Turn into well-greased corn-stick or muffin pans, filling cups about ⅔ full. Bake about 20 minutes. *Makes 12 to 15 muffins or corn sticks.*

CROISSANTS

2 packages active dry yeast	2 cups milk, scalded
½ cup warm water	7 to 8 cups sifted flour
½ cup sugar	2 eggs, well beaten
6 tablespoons butter	Melted butter
2 teaspoons salt	

Soften the yeast in the ½ cup of warm water; let stand 5 minutes. In a large bowl, mix the sugar, butter, salt, and milk; cool to lukewarm, and mix well. Add 1 cup of the flour, and beat until smooth. Add the softened yeast; mix well. Add about half of the remaining flour; beat until smooth. Beat in the eggs. Add enough remaining flour to make a soft dough. Turn out on a floured board, let stand 5 minutes, and knead 5 minutes, or until smooth and elastic. Put in a large greased bowl, turn to bring greased side up. Cover with waxed paper and a towel, and let stand in a warm place for 1½ hours, or until doubled in bulk. Punch down, cover, and let rise ½ hour as before. Turn out on lightly floured board.

Roll dough into a 12-inch circle, ¼-inch thick; brush with melted butter. Cut into 16 wedges. Roll each wedge separately, beginning at wide edge. Put on a greased baking sheet with wedges pointing underneath, and shape into crescents. Brush with melted butter. Cover and let rise about 15 minutes.

While rolls are rising, preheat the oven to 425° F.

Bake for about 15 minutes, or until browned. *Makes 16 croissants.*

Croissants freeze well and should be warmed before serving.

LITTLE LOAVES OF BREAD

1 package active dry yeast
1⅓ cups warm water
3¼ cups sifted flour
5 teaspoons sugar

1½ teaspoons salt
1 tablespoon soft
   shortening

In a large bowl, sprinkle the dry yeast into the warm water. Let stand a few minutes; then stir until dissolved. Add 1½ cups flour, sugar, salt and shortening. Beat by hand or at low speed with electric mixer until blended; then beat an additional 2 minutes by hand or at medium speed with mixer. Beat in 1¾ cups flour by hand. Cover, and let rise until doubled (about 45 minutes).

Stir down and spread evenly in 6 greased 4¾ by 2⅝ by 1½-inch pans. Smooth and shape tops of loaves with floured hand. Let rise until batter reaches tops of pans (about 20 minutes).

While the dough is rising, preheat the oven to 375° F.

Bake the loaves for about 30 minutes, or until they are done. Cool on racks. *Makes 6 small loaves; each loaf yields about 6 small slices.*

For a special touch, give each little loaf wrapped in plastic wrap on a miniature bread board.

Note: For whole-wheat breads, substitute 1¾ cups of unsifted whole-wheat flour for the white flour in the last beating step.

CARAWAY-RYE BREAD STICKS

1 package active dry yeast
1¼ cups warm water
¼ cup margarine, softened
3 tablespoons sugar
½ teaspoon salt

2 cups whole-rye flour
   Caraway seeds
2 cups all-purpose flour
1 egg yolk beaten with 1
   tablespoon milk

Dissolve the yeast in the 1¼ cups of warm water in a mixing bowl. Add the margarine, sugar, salt, whole-rye flour and 1 tablespoon of caraway seeds and beat until smooth. Cover and let rise in a warm place for about 40 minutes.

Stir in the all-purpose flour, ½ cup at a time, then turn out on a lightly floured board and knead until smooth and elastic. Divide in half and shape into 2 rolls. Cut each role into 12 equal pieces. Shape each piece into a 6-inch rope. Place on greased baking sheets, about 2 inches apart. Cover and let rise about 30 minutes.

While the sticks are rising, preheat the oven to 400° F.

Brush the sticks with the egg yolk-and-milk mixture and sprinkle with additional caraway seeds. Bake for 15 minutes, or until done. Cool on racks, covered with a kitchen towel. *Makes a dozen bread sticks.*

Store the sticks in an airtight container or freeze and reheat them to crisp them up before giving.

SEEDED BREAD SQUARES

1 package active dry yeast	¾ cup cold water
¼ cup warm water	1¼ cups nonfat dry milk
Butter	Sifted flour (about 5½
2 tablespoons salt	cups)
2 tablespoons sugar	Caraway, sesame, celery
1 cup boiling water	or poppy seeds

Soften the yeast in the ¼ cup of warm water; let it stand 5 minutes. Put 2 tablespoons of butter, the salt, sugar and 1 cup of boiling water in a large bowl; mix well and add ¾ cup cold water; cool to lukewarm. Add the yeast mixture. Sift the dry milk and flour together. Add 3 cups to the yeast mixture; beat with a spoon until smooth. Add 2 cups more of the flour mixture, or enough to make a dough that doesn't stick to the sides of the bowl and can be kneaded. Use the remaining flour mixture for kneading.

Turn the dough onto a floured board and knead for 10 minutes, or until smooth and elastic. Put in a large, greased bowl. Turn to bring greased side up. Cover with a towel and let stand in a warm place for 1½ hours, or until doubled in bulk.

Punch the dough down and divide it into 2 equal parts. Shape into square loaves and put in 2 greased 9-inch square pans. Let rise ½ hour.

Preheat the oven to 400° F. while the dough is rising.

Bake for about 25 minutes. Cool slightly on a rack. Cut each loaf into 16 cubes. Dip each cube in melted butter and then in seeds. Reduce oven heat to 375° F. Return cubes to pans and heat for 10 to 15 minutes. *Makes 32 bread squares.*

These squares can be frozen until they are given.

Cakes

WHETHER IT BE an elaborate birthday or wedding cake, a Christmas fruitcake or a simple pound cake to add to the buffet table, no gift is more festive than a beautiful cake. Especially now, when the cost of fine, fresh ingredients has forced all but the most expensive bakeries to skimp or to use cheap substitutes, a rich, homemade cake is a very special treat.

These recipes include both plain and fancy cakes, in order to meet a variety of needs.

The cake you give should be selected with an eye toward those who will be eating it and the way in which it will be served. An elaborate, frosted layer cake is wrong for a casual occasion; if you bring it as a surprise, it might compete with or overshadow your hostess's dessert. Try giving a coffee cake or an unfrosted spice cake in such situations, or whenever you feel uncertain. A birthday cake, on the other hand, should be rich and gooey, unless it's for the rare person who dislikes such confections. Cakes that can be cut and served in slices or squares, without plates, are best for picnics or buffets.

Most of these recipes are for moist cakes that keep well and do not have to be made at the last minute. Try, however, to give cakes when they are as fresh as possible. Some of these cakes require refrigeration and should only be given when you do not have far to travel. If you are making a cake the night before you plan to present it, remember that an iced cake will keep better than unfrosted layers. If you plan to keep a cake for several days before giving it, wrap it very well in foil or plastic wrap and store it in a cake saver, a deep bowl or the refrigerator. Just about all cakes freeze well: wrap the layers separately and freeze them unfrosted.

When sending a cake by mail, choose a solid, unfrosted cake, such as pound cake, fruitcake or coffee cake. Wrap it well in foil and tie it with cotton yarn or ribbon. Pack it in a sturdy box surrounded by crumpled newspaper and send it the fastest way possible.

If you are bringing someone a delicate cake, make sure that you have a good container in which to carry it. Bakeries will often give or sell you their cardboard cake boxes and you can keep a few of these on hand, unassembled so that they can be stored flat. You can also carry a cake in a styrofoam cooler or give it in a decorated hatbox. If you give cakes often, it may pay to invest in a special cake carrier. If you're bringing a cake to someone who bakes a lot, you may want to make the cake carrier part of the gift.

Tips on Baking Cakes

• Be sure you have the proper equipment. You will need measuring spoons, measuring cups, a rubber spatula, a whisk, a wooden spoon, a sifter, cake racks, mixing bowls in various sizes and a beater. A well-equipped baker's kitchen must also include baking pans in a variety of sizes: 8-inch and/or 9-inch layer pans, a 9-inch or 10-inch tube pan, an 8-inch or 9-inch square pan, a 9 by 13-inch rectangular pan, a 9 by 5 by 3-inch loaf pan, a jelly-roll pan and several baking sheets.
• Use high-quality ingredients.
• Have all the ingredients at room temperature. Measure accurately, using level measurements.
• Assemble all the ingredients before you begin to mix the cake.
• Preheat the oven thoroughly while you are mixing the cake. Be sure that your oven temperature is accurate; use an oven thermometer if you have any question.

• Use all-purpose flour, except when cake flour is specifically called for.

• Use "large" eggs in these recipes. Don't substitute eggs of another size; there *is* a difference.

• Don't double these recipes.

• Don't overbeat the batter or the cake will be dry and tough.

• Add sugar gradually to the batter.

• When dry and liquid ingredients are to be added alternately, begin and end with the dry ingredients.

• Some of these recipes call for pan liners, made of waxed or brown paper and cut slightly smaller than the bottoms of the pans so that the paper does not touch the edge. If you use pan liners it is not necessary to grease the paper or the pans. If you prefer not to use them, grease and flour the pans instead.

• Place cake pans in the center of the oven. Do not let them touch each other.

• Let cakes cool completely before icing them.

• Cakes with perishable cream fillings or frostings should always be kept in the refrigerator.

• Allow about 1 hour for a frozen cake, in its wrappings, to defrost at room temperature.

Ideas for Giving Cakes

Even if it's not a birthday cake, a gift cake should be thoughtfully decorated. Be imaginative and allow yourself enough time to fuss a bit with the cake's appearance. It will be more personal if it's decorated for a specific person, occasion or holiday.

You can decorate cakes with nuts, fruits, berries, small candies, sprinkles, fresh or candied flowers, flags or miniature toys. Messages written in icing can be funny or cryptic or sentimental, according to your mood. Ready-to-use icings for writing and decorating cakes are sold in tubes or containers at most supermarkets. You can also make your own by beating an egg white with enough confectioners' sugar to reach the proper consistency, and then squeezing it through a pastry bag.

Plain cakes can be glazed and decorated. You can prepare a

simple glaze by melting currant jelly or by mixing equal parts of honey or corn syrup and water, boiling it for a few minutes and brushing it warm on a cold cake. You can make a simple frosting by beating an egg white with a cup of confectioners' sugar and a few drops of almond or other extract or by melting semisweet chocolate with a little honey and a few drops of water.

Glazed dried fruits such as prunes or apricots make attractive decorations. Simmer them, covered, in water for about 10 minutes and then drain them. Mix equal parts of honey, water and sugar and bring the mixture to a boil. Add the drained fruits and simmer them about 15 minutes. The fruits can be used to decorate a cake and the liquid to glaze it.

Use candied cherries and nuts to decorate a Christmas cake. Leaves can be cut from citron, angelica or green candied pineapple. You can press slices of green and red candied pineapple into the glaze, or use red cinnamon candies and green gumdrops. There are tiny candy canes and lots of other small Christmas candies to use as cake decorations.

If you wish, you can give a cake on a pretty paper plate and add a cake server or a cake knife to your gift. Or present the cake on a handsome ceramic plate or wooden tray. If the cake is plain, make a special sauce to go with it (pp. 138–48) and bring it in a separate container. Give coffee cake with a jar of coffee beans, pound cake with special tea or tea bags. For very important occasions, like a wedding, present the cake on a raised-pedestal cake stand. Cellophane, plastic wrap, foil or tissue paper make the best wrappings for cakes.

APPLESAUCE CAKE

½ cup shortening	½ teaspoon baking soda
1 cup packed light brown sugar	½ teaspoon salt
1 cup applesauce	1 teaspoon baking powder
2¼ cups flour	¾ teaspoon apple-pie spice
	1 cup chopped nuts

Preheat the oven to 325° F.

Cream the shortening and sugar together in a large bowl. Add the applesauce. Sift together the flour, soda, salt, baking powder and spice. Add to the first mixture. Fold in the nuts. Bake in a greased 9 by 5 by 3-inch loaf pan for 1 hour. Frost when cool, if you wish.

This moist cake will keep well and is easy to transport.

BÛCHE DE NOËL

3 eggs
⅔ cup sugar
4 tablespoons cornstarch
2 tablespoons cocoa
1 teaspoon baking powder
¼ teaspoon salt
Confectioners' sugar

¼ cup finely chopped nuts
¼ cup finely chopped candied orange peel
1 cup heavy cream, whipped
Chopped pistachios

CHOCOLATE FROSTING

2 squares unsweetened chocolate
½ cup softened butter or margarine

2 teaspoons vanilla extract
2 cups confectioners' sugar
2 tablespoons milk

Line a 15 by 10 by 1-inch jelly-roll pan with well-greased waxed paper, leaving a 2-inch overhang at each end of the pan.

Preheat the oven to 400° F.

In the large bowl of an electric mixer beat the eggs until foamy; gradually add the sugar and continue mixing about 10 minutes, or until very thick and lemon-colored. Sift together the cornstarch, cocoa, baking powder and salt; sift again into egg mixture and fold, blending well. Spread batter in prepared pan and bake for 8 to 10 minutes, or until a pick inserted in the center comes out clean (do not overbake).

Loosen edges with a spatula, lift cake from the pan by paper ends and invert on a kitchen towel sprinkled with confectioners' sugar. Remove paper. Cool 5 minutes, then roll from narrow end with towel in between. Cool on a rack.

Fold the chopped nuts and the orange peel into the cream. Unroll cake and spread with cream mixture; reroll without towel. Place on a serving dish and frost, making decorative grooves with a small spatula. Decorate with chopped pistachios. Chill for at least 30 minutes.

Chocolate Frosting: Melt the chocolate over hot water; remove from heat. Cream the butter until light and fluffy; blend in chocolate and vanilla. Gradually beat in the confectioners' sugar alternately with the milk until smooth.

This cake should be kept in the refrigerator and given only when you do not have far to travel.

CHOCOLATE SEVEN-LAYER CAKE

6 eggs, separated	¾ cup sifted flour
1¼ cups sugar	¼ cup cornstarch
2 tablespoons lemon juice	½ teaspoon salt

CHOCOLATE FROSTING

2 (12-ounce) packages semisweet chocolate chips	½ cup soft butter
	2 teaspoons vanilla extract
4 cups sifted confectioners' sugar	About ½ cup hot milk

Preheat the oven to 450° F.

Beat the egg yolks until thick. Gradually add the sugar, beating constantly with a rotary beater; add half of the lemon juice. Add sifted dry ingredients alternately with remaining lemon juice, beating until smooth. Fold in stiffly beaten egg whites.

Spread a few tablespoons of batter in each of 2 or 3 8-inch layer pans, lined on the bottom with paper. Bake 5 minutes. Turn out on racks. Repeat the baking process until all the batter is used and 7 layers are baked.

Frost between the layers and on top and sides of cake. Chill.
Chocolate Frosting: Melt the chocolate over hot water. Beat
in the sugar, butter, vanilla and enough of the milk to make
the frosting of good spreading consistency. Beat until smooth.

This cake will keep well in the refrigerator and can also be
frozen.

CHOCOLATE SHADOW CAKE

6 squares unsweetened chocolate	3 eggs
½ cup hot water	2 cups sifted cake flour
1¾ cups sugar	1 teaspoon soda
Soft butter or margarine	½ teaspoon salt
1 teaspoon vanilla extract	⅔ cup milk

FLUFFY WHITE FROSTING

2 egg whites	⅓ cup water
1½ cups sugar	2 teaspoons light corn syrup
⅛ teaspoon salt	1 teaspoon vanilla

Preheat the oven at 350° F.

Melt 4 squares of chocolate in the hot water in the top part
of a double boiler over boiling water. Cook until thickened,
stirring. Add ½ cup sugar, and cook 2 or 3 minutes, stirring.
Cool.

Cream ½ cup butter and the remaining 1¼ cups sugar. Add
the vanilla. Add the eggs, one at a time, beating thoroughly
after each addition. Add sifted dry ingredients alternately with
the milk, beating until smooth. Add the chocolate mixture, and
blend.

Pour into 2 9-inch layer pans, lined on bottom with paper.
Bake about 45 minutes. Cool and frost. When frosting is set,
melt 2 squares of chocolate and 2 teaspoons of butter. Dribble
over top of cake. Let chocolate set.

Fluffy White Frosting: In the top part of a small double

boiler, combine the egg whites, sugar, salt, water and corn syrup. Beat with electric beater over boiling water for 7 minutes, until mixture stands in stiff peaks. Add the vanilla.

CHOCOLATE-WALNUT BUTTER CAKE

¾ cup chopped walnuts
3 cups flour
½ cup unsweetened cocoa
¼ teaspoon salt
1 teaspoon baking powder
1 cup softened butter

½ cup shortening
2 cups granulated sugar
5 eggs
1 cup milk
2 teaspoons vanilla extract
Confectioners' sugar

Grease a 10 by 4-inch tube pan and sprinkle the bottom with ¼ cup of finely chopped walnuts; set aside.

Preheat the oven to 325° F.

Sift the flour, cocoa, salt and baking powder together and set aside. Cream the butter and the shortening. Gradually add the sugar and beat until fluffy. Add the eggs, one at a time, beating well after each. Add the dry ingredients alternately with the milk and the vanilla. Add the remaining ½ cup of chopped walnuts and mix well.

Put the batter in the tube pan and bake for 1 hour and 20 minutes, or until done. Let rest on a rack for 5 minutes before turning out. Cool, wrap well and store in a cool place.

A few days' storing will improve the flavor of this cake. It also freezes well. Dust it with confectioners' sugar before giving.

CHRISTMAS COFFEE WREATHS

FILLING

¼ cup softened butter or
   margarine
¾ cup confectioners' sugar
2 teaspoons grated orange
   rind

¾ cup finely chopped pecans,
   walnuts, filberts or
   almonds

DOUGH

6 cups flour
½ cup sugar
1 teaspoon salt
3 packages active dry yeast
½ cup butter or margarine,
   softened

1 cup hot water
4 eggs, 3 at room
   temperature

DECORATION

Confectioners' sugar
Red or green candied
   pineapple and cherries

Prepare the filling first: Cream the butter and add the sugar,
orange rind and nuts. Mix well and set aside while preparing
the dough.

In the large bowl of an electric mixer, combine 2 cups of the
flour, the sugar, salt, yeast and butter. Gradually add 1 cup of
hot water (120° to 130° F.) and beat, scraping bowl occasionally, for 2 minutes. Add 3 eggs and ½ cup of flour. Beat at high
speed, scraping bowl occasionally, for 2 minutes. Stir in enough
additional flour to make a soft dough.

Turn out on a lightly floured board and knead 5 minutes, or
until smooth and elastic. Divide dough in half and shape each
half into a round ball. Roll 1 ball into a 16-inch circle. With a
pastry wheel or sharp knife, cut the circle into 12 triangles.
Using half the filling, put about 1 teaspoonful on each triangle.
Shape into crescents, starting at base of triangle. Bring two ends
of crescents together and pinch. Repeat with remaining half
of dough. (The crescents can be frozen at this point for up to
4 weeks until you are ready to bake them.)

Arrange each set of 12 crescents with sides touching on a
baking sheet in the shape of a wreath. Thaw, lightly covered,
and let rise in a warm place free from drafts for 2 hours, or until
doubled.

While dough is rising, preheat the oven to 375° F.

Brush each wreath with beaten egg and bake them for 20 to

25 minutes. Loosen with a spatula and remove to racks to cool. Sprinkle confectioners' sugar on them and decorate them with candied fruits.

HUNGARIAN COFFEE CAKE

1 package active dry yeast
¼ cup warm water
¾ cup milk, scalded and
    cooled
1 cup sugar
1 teaspoon salt

1 egg
¾ cup butter or margarine
3½ cups (about) flour
1 teaspoon cinnamon
¾ cup finely chopped nuts
4 tablespoons raisins

Sprinkle the yeast on the ¼ cup of warm water. Let stand a few minutes, then stir until dissolved. Add the milk, ¼ cup of sugar, the salt, egg, ¼ cup of softened butter and half the flour. Beat with a spoon until smooth. Gradually add enough more flour to make a stiff dough. Turn out on a lightly floured board and knead for 5 minutes, or until smooth and elastic. Put in a greased bowl and turn greased side up. Cover and let rise in a warm place for 1½ hours, or until doubled. Punch down and let rise again for 30 minutes, or until almost doubled.

Cut dough in pieces the size of walnuts and shape into balls. Roll the balls in the remaining butter, melted, then roll in a mixture of the remaining sugar, the cinnamon and nuts. Put a layer of balls barely touching in a well-greased 9- or 10-inch tube pan (if bottom is removable, line with foil). Sprinkle with 2 tablespoons of raisins. Add another layer of balls and sprinkle with remaining raisins, pressing in slightly. Let rise about 45 minutes.

While the dough is rising, preheat the oven to 350° F.

If any cinnamon mixture remains, sprinkle on top. Bake for 35 to 40 minutes. Loosen from pan and invert so butter-sugar mixture runs down over cake.

Wrap well if you plan to keep the cake for a day or two before giving it. Enclose a note, saying that the cake can be reheated and served warm, if desired.

BROWN-SUGAR FUDGE CAKE

½ cup soft butter or
    margarine
2¼ cups sifted cake flour
1 teaspoon baking soda
¾ teaspoon salt
2 cups light brown sugar,
    packed

1 cup buttermilk
1 teaspoon vanilla extract
3 eggs
3 squares unsweetened
    chocolate, melted

CARAMEL FROSTING
2 cups packed light brown
    sugar
1 cup granulated sugar
2 tablespoons light corn
    syrup

3 tablespoons butter
Dash of salt
⅔ cup cream
1 teaspoon vanilla

DECORATION
Walnut or pecan halves

Preheat the oven to 350° F.

Cream the butter. Sift the flour, baking soda and salt onto butter. Add the sugar, ⅔ cup of buttermilk and vanilla. Beat 2 minutes. Add the remaining ⅓ cup of buttermilk, the eggs and cooled chocolate. Beat 2 minutes.

Pour into 2 9-inch layer pans, lined on bottom with paper. Bake about 30 minutes. Cool, frost and decorate with nuts.

Caramel Frosting: In a large saucepan, mix the brown sugar, granulated sugar, corn syrup, butter, salt, cream and vanilla. Bring to a boil, cover and cook for 3 minutes. Uncover and cook until a small amount of mixture forms a soft ball when dropped into cold water (236° F. on a candy thermometer).

Cool 5 minutes; then beat until thick. If too stiff, add a little hot water.

BLOND FRUITCAKE

Grated rind of 1 lemon
1 cup chopped mixed
candied fruits
½ cup each currants, golden
raisins and chopped
pecans or walnuts
2¼ cups sifted cake flour
1½ teaspoons baking powder

1 package (8 ounces)
cream cheese, slightly
softened
1 cup butter, slightly
softened
1½ cups granulated sugar
4 large eggs

DECORATION
Glaze (see introduction to
cakes, p. 69)

Confectioners' sugar
Candied fruits

Butter a 10-inch bundt or tube pan and set aside. Combine the lemon rind, fruits and nuts and set aside. Sift the flour with the baking powder and set aside.

Preheat the oven to 325° F.

Beat the cream cheese and butter until fluffy. Gradually beat in the granulated sugar. Add the eggs one at a time, beating well after each. Gradually add the flour-and-baking powder mixture and stir until well blended.

Fold the fruit-nut mixture into the batter and pour into pan. Bake for 1 hour and 20 minutes, or until done. Let stand in pan on rack for 5 minutes, then turn out on rack to cool.

Glaze or decorate with confectioners' sugar and candied fruits before giving.

Wrapped and refrigerated, preferably in an airtight container, light fruitcakes will keep for about 2 weeks. They can also be frozen. Do not put liquor on white fruitcakes because it may make them soggy.

DARK FRUITCAKE

1½ cups packed brown sugar
4 eggs, separated
3 cups all-purpose flour
1 teaspoon baking powder
2 teaspoons salt
1 tablespoon cinnamon
1 teaspoon allspice
1 teaspoon ground cloves
1 cup fruit juice
¾ pound citron, shaved

½ pound candied pineapple, chopped
1 pound candied cherries, halved
½ pound dried figs, chopped
1 cup raisins
1 pound nuts, chopped (about 4 cups)
1 cup butter, melted, or vegetable oil

Mix the sugar and egg yolks vigorously for 2 minutes. Sift 2 cups of flour with the baking powder, salt and spices. Add to first mixture alternately with the fruit juice, mixing until smooth. Fold in stiffly beaten egg whites. Mix the remaining flour with the fruits and nuts, coating well. Add to first mixture with the butter and mix well.

Preheat the oven to 275° F.

Press the batter into 2 9 by 5 by 3-inch loaf pans, lined on the bottom with waxed paper. Bake very slowly for about 4 hours. *Makes 2 fruitcakes.* Allow the cakes to age a week or two before giving.

Wrapped and refrigerated, preferably in an airtight container, dark fruitcakes will keep for several months. They keep better than light ones because the larger proportion of fruits to batter adds moisture. Wrap them first with a cloth soaked in brandy, wine or bourbon, if you wish. They may also be frozen.

MINCEMEAT CAKE

½ cup soft butter or
    margarine
1⅓ cups sugar
  2 eggs
  1 cup moist mincemeat
  2 cups sifted flour
  2 teaspoons baking powder

½ teaspoon salt
⅓ cup milk
2 tablespoons molasses
⅓ cup chopped nuts
½ cup diced watermelon
    preserves

Preheat the oven to 350° F.

Cream the butter and sugar until light. Add the eggs, one at a time, beating well after each addition. Warm the mincemeat slightly; beat into first mixture. Add sifted flour, baking powder and salt alternately with combined milk and molasses, beating until smooth. Fold in the nuts and preserves. Pour into two 8-inch layer pans, lined on the bottom with paper. Bake for 35 minutes.

Wrapped in foil or plastic wrap, this moist cake will keep well in the refrigerator.

GEORGIA PECAN CAKE

3¾ cups flour
  1 teaspoon baking powder
  4 teaspoons nutmeg
  1 cup butter or margarine,
    softened
  2 cups sugar

6 large eggs
4 cups coarsely chopped
  pecans
5 cups golden raisins
½ cup brandy, wine or
  orange juice

DECORATION
Candied cherries

Pecan halves

Preheat the oven to 275° F.

Put the flour, baking powder and nutmeg in a bowl and mix well with a fork.

In a separate bowl, cream the butter until fluffy. Gradually add the sugar, continuing to cream. Add the eggs, two at a time, beating well after each addition. Mix ½ cup of the dry ingredients with the nuts and raisins and set aside. Add the remainder of the dry ingredients to the creamed mixture alternately with the brandy, mixing after each addition until well blended. Add the coated nuts and raisins and mix in lightly but thoroughly.

Put the batter in a large tube pan or two 9 by 5 by 3-inch loaf pans. Bake, allowing about 2 hours for a tube cake and 1½ hours for loaves. Let stand in pans on racks for about 15 minutes, then turn out on racks and cool completely. Decorate with candied cherries and pecan halves.

Wrap well and store in a cool place up to 2 weeks.

GINGER POUND CAKE

1 cup butter or margarine,
    softened
2 cups packed light brown
    sugar
4 eggs, separated
3 cups flour
1 teaspoon baking powder

1 teaspoon nutmeg
1 tablespoon ground ginger
1 teaspoon salt
2 tablespoons minced
    candied ginger
½ cup light cream

Preheat the oven to 350° F.

Cream the butter. Gradually add the sugar and beat until light. Add the egg yolks one at a time, beating thoroughly after each. Sift together the dry ingredients and add the candied ginger. Add to first mixture alternately with the cream, blending well. Fold in stiffly beaten egg whites. Put in a 9-inch tube pan lined on the bottom with waxed paper. Bake about 1 hour. Turn out on a rack and peel off the paper.

SOUR-CREAM POUND CAKE

1 cup soft butter	1 cup sour cream
2¾ cups sugar	1 teaspoon lemon, orange
6 eggs	or vanilla flavoring
3 cups sifted flour	2 cups confectioners' sugar
½ teaspoon salt	Strawberries or blue-
¼ teaspoon baking soda	berries (optional)

Preheat the oven to 350° F.

Cream the butter and the sugar until light. Add the eggs, one at a time, beating thoroughly after each. Sift together the flour, salt and baking soda three times and add alternately with the sour cream to the first mixture, beating until smooth. Add the flavoring.

Pour the batter into a 9-inch tube pan, lined on the bottom with paper. Bake 1 hour and 20 minutes, or until done. Let stand in pan for about 5 minutes, then turn out on a rack, peel off the paper and cool.

Thin confectioners' sugar with enough water to make a thin glaze and flavor it with the same flavoring as you used in the cake, or with one of the other flavorings, if you wish. Cover the top of the cake with the glaze, allowing it to run down the sides.

Store the cake, well wrapped, in an airtight container. Decorate it with berries, if you wish, before giving.

SAND CAKE

1 cup flour	1 cup sugar
1 cup cornstarch	Grated peel of 1 lemon
2 teaspoons baking powder	2 tablespoons brandy
½ teaspoon salt	6 eggs, separated
1 cup butter or margarine, softened	

Preheat the oven to 350° F.

Sift together the flour, cornstarch, baking powder and salt. In the large bowl of an electric mixer, cream the butter; gradually add the sugar and continue to cream until light and fluffy. Beat in the peel and brandy; add egg yolks one at a time, beating well after each. Continue beating, gradually adding the sifted dry ingredients. Beat egg whites until stiff but not dry; gently fold into batter. Turn into greased 10-inch tube pan and bake 45 minutes. Cool pan on a rack 5 minutes, then turn cake out on rack to cool.

OLD-FASHIONED SPICE CAKE

½ cup shortening
1 cup granulated sugar
3 eggs
1⅓ cups all-purpose flour
1 teaspoon baking soda
½ teaspoon salt
2 teaspoons cinnamon
1 teaspoon each ginger and
    ground cloves

1 teaspoon crushed cardamom seed (optional)
1 cup sour cream
Fine, dry breadcrumbs
Confectioners' sugar
    (optional)

Preheat the oven to 325° F.

Cream the shortening. Gradually add the granulated sugar and beat well. Add eggs one at a time, beating thoroughly after each. Add sifted dry ingredients, except cardamom, alternately with sour cream, blending well. Add cardamom, if desired. Grease well a 2-quart fluted tube pan, sprinkle with crumbs and shake out excess. Put batter in pan and bake about 50 minutes. Let cool in pan on rack 10 minutes before turning out. Cool and sprinkle with confectioners' sugar, if desired.

Cookies and
Small Cakes

A LMOST EVERYONE LOVES little cakes and cookies. No matter how many you make, there are never enough—the sign of a truly welcome gift. And almost all cookies freeze well. You can make them when you're in the mood and always have them on hand. They're perfect whatever the occasion: give some to your child's favorite teacher on the last day of school; bake some for a charity cake sale; bring some to a sick friend or to an informal meeting or a card party. If you don't know what to buy for a teen-aged boy, try packaging an extra-large personal supply of cookies specifically for him; he's sure to love it.

If you must send cookies or small cakes by mail, choose those that will stay fresh for at least a week. Make sure they are thick and firm enough so that they won't easily break or crumble. Pack them in tightly sealed tins or sturdy boxes. Separate each layer with waxed paper and fill in the spaces with shredded newspaper, crumpled tissue paper or popcorn. Mark the package "fragile" and send it in the fastest way possible.

Tips on Cookie Making

• Assemble and measure all the ingredients before starting to mix cookie dough.
• Use the kind of shortening called for in the recipe, softened to room temperature but not runny. Don't use whipped butter or soft margarine.

- Use "large" eggs.
- Use unsifted flour unless otherwise specified; pile it lightly in a cup and level it off.
- Make cookies the size that is suggested.
- Don't double the recipe unless it says you can.
- Preheat the oven; use an oven thermometer to make sure the temperature is accurate.
- Keep cookie doughs covered and chilled until ready to bake.
- It is not necessary to grease cookie sheets unless the recipe says that you should.
- Use cookie sheets at least 2 inches narrower and shorter than the oven rack so that heat can circulate.
- Try to use either the whole baking sheet or an inverted pie pan for the last batch.
- It is not necessary to wash cookie sheets between baking batches of cookies. If they have been greased, wipe them off with a slightly greased paper towel, brushing off any crumbs at the same time.
- Cool the sheets before reusing them or cookies will lose their shape.
- Bake cookies in the center of the oven. Watch them closely while they are baking and check for doneness shortly before the minimum baking time is up. If some cookies are thinner than others, you may have to remove them and bake the others a bit longer.
- If cookies are baking unevenly, you may have to turn the pan or move them to a higher or lower oven rack.
- When cookies are done, remove them immediately from the pans and let them cool on racks.
- Let cookies cool completely before stacking or storing them.
- Store cookies in airtight containers in a cool, dry place, or freeze them, if you prefer. Just about all cookies freeze well.
- After defrosting cookies, crisp them, if necessary, by putting them in a preheated 300° F. oven for a minute or two.

Ideas for Giving Cookies and Small Cakes

You can make cookies in many different shapes, using cookie cutters or forming them by hand to suit the season or the occasion. Christmas trees, Santas, angels, bells, wreaths and stars are traditional for Christmas; hearts and flowers for Valentine's Day; bunnies for Easter; flags for Independence Day. Bring cookies in animal shapes to an animal lover, and cookies shaped like a house to a house-warming party.

You can personalize cookies and small cakes by writing names or greetings on them. Write in icing, using the decorator icings that come in tubes or mixing an egg white with confectioners' sugar until it's stiff enough to push through a pastry bag.

Cookies and small cakes can be decorated with tinted icings, garnished with nuts, raisins or candies, or sprinkled with colored sugars. Or you can make a depression in the center of each cookie before you bake it and fill it with jam or jelly, candied ginger, candied orange or lemon peel or chocolate bits. You can also bake indented cookies and fill them *after* baking with chocolate frosting, topped with a blanched almond half.

Make Christmas cookies a family affair. There's nothing like good-natured competition to produce amusing and original creations, or a yearly tradition to hold a family together.

Some Christmas cookies can be used as tree ornaments: decorate them and hang them with yarn or string from holes which have been baked into them. (See recipes for Ornamental Sugar Cookies, pp. 106–108.) Just about any cookie will become a Christmas cookie if you decorate it with red and green sugars, with halves of red or green candied cherries or with red cinnamon candies, gumdrops or other small candies. You can make red- or green-tinted coconut by putting ½ cup of coconut, ½ teaspoon of water and a few drops of red or green food coloring in a jar, covering it and shaking it very well.

Large cookies or squares are pretty when wrapped individually in colored foil, plastic or cellophane. Save colorful candy wrappers from commercial candies and reuse them for your own goodies. Wrap Scotch Shortbread in plaid paper, Christmas cookies in red or green foil.

Save fruitcake or cookie tins and use them to package gift cookies or small cakes. You can paint large coffee tins, if you wish, or decorate them with self-adhesive paper or with seasonal ornaments such as Christmas greens, red Valentine hearts on paper doilies, or fall leaves and dried straw flowers for Thanksgiving or Halloween.

Give cookies in pretty cannisters, in glass cookie jars, in a large ceramic mixing bowl, a soufflé dish, a mold or a tall apothecary jar. Children will be delighted with cookies that come packed in a lunchbox or a plastic pail.

Cupcakes can be given right in a new cupcake pan; squares or bars in the proper-sized baking pan. If you wish, add a wooden spoon, some cookie cutters, a pastry brush or a bunch of cinnamon sticks or vanilla beans to your gift. A hand-written recipe for the cookies or cakes is always a nice touch, especially when you are giving ingredients or baking utensils along with the gift.

Pack small cookies into plastic berry baskets, woven with bright ribbon or lined with tissue paper. Or put them in plastic bags tied with yarn or lace or on a pretty paper plate, covered with clear plastic wrap.

ALMOND-LACE COOKIES

1 cup finely chopped blanched almonds	½ cup sugar
	2 tablespoons flour
½ cup butter or margarine, softened	2 tablespoons milk

Preheat the oven to 350° F.

Put the almonds, butter, sugar, flour and milk in a saucepan and cook, stirring, over medium heat just until the butter melts and the ingredients are well blended. Drop by level measuring-teaspoonfuls onto greased and floured cookie sheets, leaving a

3-inch space between cookies. Bake 5 to 6 minutes, or until lightly browned and glossy. Cool on sheets a few minutes until firm enough to remove to racks.

Store in an airtight container in a cool place with waxed paper or plastic wrap between layers. *Makes about 4 dozen.*

OLD-FASHIONED APPLE COOKIES

½ cup butter, softened
1⅓ cups packed brown sugar
1 egg
¼ cup apple juice
1 cup finely chopped, peeled, cored apples
2 cups whole-wheat pastry flour

½ teaspoon salt
1 teaspoon baking soda
½ teaspoon ground cloves
1 teaspoon cinnamon
1 cup unsulfured raisins
1 cup chopped walnuts or other nuts

GLAZE (OPTIONAL)
Mix together the following:
½ cup confectioners' sugar
1 tablespoon softened butter

2 tablespoons apple juice

Preheat the oven to 375° F.

Cream the butter and sugar until blended. Add the egg and beat well. Beat in the juice. Add the apples, flour, salt, baking soda and cloves and mix well. Fold in the cinnamon, raisins and nuts and drop by rounded teaspoonfuls about 2 inches apart onto greased cookie sheets.

Bake about 13 minutes. Cool on racks and, if you wish, brush with Glaze while still warm. *Makes 4 dozen.*

APRICOT-FILLED PINWHEELS

APRICOT FILLING
1 cup dried apricots   ⅓ cup sugar
¾ cup water

PASTRY
2 cups flour   ½ teaspoon white vinegar
1 cup margarine, softened   1 egg yolk beaten with 1
⅓ cup ice water   tablespoon milk

Apricot Filling: Put the apricots and water in a small pot and bring them to a boil over medium heat. Stir in the sugar, cover and simmer until the apricots are tender, about 15 minutes. Puree in a blender until smooth or press through a food mill. Chill until ready to use.

Prepare the pastry by putting the flour in a mixing bowl and cutting in the margarine with a pastry blender or a fork until the mixture looks like cornmeal. Combine the ice water and vinegar and sprinkle over the flour mixture, quickly gather into a ball, then flatten out on waxed paper to a rectangle. Wrap and chill for 1 hour.

Preheat the oven to 425° F.

Divide the dough in half. On a lightly floured board, roll each half into a 12 by 9-inch rectangle; trim the edges with a sharp knife or pastry wheel and cut into 3-inch squares. Slit each corner of each square 1¼ inches from the tip toward the center. Drop 1 teaspoonful of filling in the center and fold every other tip to the center like a pinwheel; pinch firmly in the center.

Place on a baking sheet; brush with the egg yolk-milk mixture. Bake for 12 minutes, or until lightly browned. Cool on a rack, then store in a cool place. *Makes about 24.*

BABAS AU RHUM

1 package active dry yeast	¼ cup sugar
¼ cup warm water	1 egg
¼ cup milk	Grated rind ½ lemon
¼ cup butter or margarine	⅛ teaspoon salt
2 egg yolks	1¾ cups sifted flour

RUM SYRUP

1½ cups water	1 stick cinnamon
1½ cups sugar	1 whole clove
½ sliced lemon	¾ cup dark rum
1 slice orange	

Soften the yeast in the ¼ cup of warm water and set aside. Scald the milk, add the butter and stir until melted; cool to lukewarm. In a large bowl, beat the egg yolks well; gradually add the sugar and continue beating. Beat in the whole egg. Add the milk mixture, the yeast mixture, lemon rind and salt. Gradually add the flour, beating until smooth. Cover and let rise in a warm place until doubled.

While the batter is rising, make the *Rum Syrup:* Mix the water, sugar, lemon, orange, cinnamon and clove in a small pot; simmer 5 minutes; strain and stir in the rum. Set aside.

When the batter has fully risen, stir it down. Spoon it into greased small muffin pans, about ⅔ full. Let rise until the batter reaches the top.

While the batter is rising, preheat the oven to 350° F.

Bake about 10 minutes; cool. Place in a shallow dish and cover with Rum Syrup. Baste several times, so that each one is soaked. Cover and refrigerate. Give in an attractive, lidded jar. *Makes 24 to 36.*

BASLER BRUNSLI

These are Swiss confections, named for the city of Basel.

1 cup sugar	2 tablespoons kirsch
1 cup ground almonds	1 teaspoon cinnamon
½ cup grated unsweetened chocolate	¼ teaspoon cloves
	2 egg whites

Combine all ingredients, except the egg whites. Beat the whites until almost stiff. Add the almond-chocolate mixture and work all together to form a dough. Roll or pat to about a 1-inch thickness on a board lightly sprinkled with sugar, and cut into rosettes (the traditional shape) or into 1½-inch circles. Put on a greased sheet; let dry 2 or 3 hours.

Preheat the oven to 325° F. Bake for 10 to 15 minutes. *Makes 18.*

BOURBON BROWNIES

⅓ cup margarine	¾ cup flour
2 squares (2 ounces) unsweetened chocolate	¼ teaspoon salt
½ teaspoon vanilla extract	3 tablespoons (about) bourbon
1 cup sugar	Tinted almonds
2 eggs	

Preheat the oven to 325° F.

Melt the margarine and chocolate in a saucepan over low heat, stirring; cool. Beat in the vanilla and sugar. Add the eggs, one at a time, beating well after each. Mix the flour and salt and stir into the chocolate mixture. Spread in a greased 8-inch square pan. Bake about 25 minutes; cool.

When thoroughly cooled, crumble brownies into a bowl. Sprinkle with bourbon; mix in with your fingers. Shape into 1-inch balls or logs about 1 inch long. Roll in tinted almonds, made by mixing a few drops of food coloring with ¼ teaspoon water and sprinkling it on finely chopped blanched almonds.

Store these brownies in an airtight container for a day before giving. *Makes 3 to 3½ dozen.*

CHEWY WHEAT-GERM BROWNIES

4 squares unsweetened chocolate	1 cup wheat germ
¾ cup margarine	2 cups sugar
1¼ cups all-purpose flour	3 eggs, well beaten
2 teaspoons baking powder	1 teaspoon vanilla extract
1 teaspoon salt	1 cup coarsely chopped walnuts

Preheat the oven to 350° F.

Melt the chocolate and margarine in a small saucepan and set aside. In a large bowl, combine the flour, baking powder, salt, wheat germ and sugar and mix well. Stir in the melted chocolate mixture, the eggs and vanilla and mix well. Fold in the nuts and spread in a greased 13 by 9 by 2-inch pan.

Bake for about 30 minutes. Cool and cut into squares. *Makes 24 to 30 brownies.*

These brownies keep well in an airtight container. They may also be frozen.

BRANDY ROLLUPS

½ cup unsulfured molasses	⅔ cup sugar
½ cup butter, softened	1 tablespoon ground ginger
1¼ cups all-purpose flour	3 tablespoons brandy
¼ teaspoon salt	

Preheat the oven to 300° F.

Bring the molasses to a boil in a saucepan. Add the butter and stir until melted. Mix together the flour, salt, sugar and ginger and gradually add to the molasses mixture. Add the brandy and stir until well mixed. Drop by level measuring-teaspoonfuls 3 inches apart onto a greased cookie sheet, baking only 6 to 8 at a time. Bake for 10 minutes.

Cool 1 minute, then remove with a wide spatula and roll at once around the handle of a wooden spoon. Press where cookie overlaps. (If removed from pan too soon, wafer will shrink; if not soon enough, wafer will be too brittle to roll. If too brittle, put back in the oven a few minutes to soften again.) Repeat until all of the mixture is used, lightly greasing the cookie sheet each time. *Makes about 3½ dozen.*

Store in an airtight container. Can be frozen. These cookies are not good shippers—they break easily.

CAROB-NUT COOKIES

1 cup all-purpose flour	6 tablespoons brown sugar
2 tablespoons raw wheat germ	½ teaspoon vanilla extract
½ teaspoon baking soda	1 egg
½ teaspoon salt	1 package (6 ounces) carob
½ cup butter, softened	nuggets or 1 6-ounce
6 tablespoons granulated sugar	carob candy bar, coarsely chopped
	½ cup coarsely chopped nuts

Preheat the oven to 375° F.

Mix together the flour, wheat germ, baking soda and salt and set aside. Cream the butter with the two sugars. Add the vanilla and egg and beat well. Add the dry ingredients and mix thoroughly. Stir in the carob and nuts and drop by teaspoonfuls 2 inches apart onto ungreased cookie sheets.

Bake for 10 to 12 minutes. Remove at once and cool on racks. *Makes about 4 dozen.*

CENCI

The Italian Santa Claus brings these to good children.

3 eggs	1½ teaspoons baking powder
2 tablespoons granulated sugar	1½ teaspoons softened butter
½ teaspoon salt	Fat for frying
½ teaspoon vanilla extract	2 tablespoons confectioners' sugar
½ teaspoon almond extract	⅛ teaspoon cinnamon
2 cups flour	

Beat the eggs, granulated sugar and salt until frothy. Add vanilla and almond extracts. Sift the flour with the baking powder. Add gradually to egg mixture. Add the butter. Mix well. Turn out on a lightly floured board and knead about 10 minutes. Divide dough in half. Roll to noodle thinness. Cut in ¾-inch strips with a fluted pastry wheel. Fry in hot, deep fat (370° F. on a frying thermometer) about 1 minute. Drain; sprinkle with mixed confectioners' sugar and cinnamon. *Makes 4 dozen.*

CHOCOLATE-COCONUT COOKIES

¾ cup butter, softened	¼ teaspoon cinnamon
1 cup packed light brown sugar	¼ teaspoon nutmeg
1 egg	¼ teaspoon salt
1 teaspoon vanilla extract	1 bag (7 ounces) cookie coconut
½ teaspoon almond extract	4 squares semisweet chocolate
2¼ cups flour	1 teaspoon rum flavoring
¾ teaspoon baking powder	

Cream the butter. Gradually add the sugar and cream until light and fluffy. Beat in the egg and flavorings. Mix the flour, baking powder, spices and salt and stir into the butter mixture. Mix in the coconut. Divide in half. Roll each half between 2 sheets of waxed paper to a rectangle 10½ inches by 9 inches and chill for 1 hour.

Preheat the oven to 375° F.

Cut the dough lengthwise in 1-inch-wide strips and crosswise in 1½-inch pieces. Put on an ungreased cookie sheet. Press ridges in each with a floured fork. Bake 7 to 8 minutes. Cool on a wire rack.

Melt the chocolate over hot water and add the rum flavoring. Dip one end of each cookie in melted chocolate. *Makes about 10 dozen.*

SPICY CHOCOLATE REFRIGERATOR COOKIES

Prepare the dough for these cookies the day before baking them.

½ cup butter or margarine, softened	1¾ cups flour
¾ cup sugar	¼ cup unsweetened cocoa
1 egg	½ teaspoon baking powder
¾ cup nuts, ground in blender	½ teaspoon cinnamon
	¼ teaspoon ground cloves
	Multicolored candies

Cream the butter and sugar together until light. Beat in the egg, then add the nuts. Mix together the flour, cocoa, baking powder, cinnamon and cloves and stir into the first mixture. Divide the dough into two equal parts and shape each into a roll about 1 inch in diameter. Sprinkle the crushed candies on waxed paper and coat each roll. Wrap the rolls in waxed paper and chill overnight.

The next day, preheat the oven to 350° F.

Cut the cookie dough into ¼-inch slices and bake on lightly greased cookie sheets for about 10 minutes. *Makes about 5 dozen.*

CINNAMON-NUT SQUARES

1 cup butter or margarine, softened	1 tablespoon cinnamon
1 cup sugar	¼ teaspoon salt
1 egg, separated	1 cup finely chopped pecans,
2 cups flour	filberts or unblanched almonds

Preheat the oven to 300° F.

Cream the butter; gradually add the sugar and continue creaming until light and fluffy. Add the egg yolk, flour, cinnamon and salt and mix well. Spread in a buttered 15 by 10 by 1-inch pan. Brush with lightly beaten egg white and sprinkle with nuts, then press nuts into surface. Bake for about 50 minutes. Cut into 48 squares while still hot.

Store these squares in an airtight container in a cool place. They keep well and are excellent for shipping.

JAMAICAN COCONUT SQUARES

¼ cup butter	½ teaspoon salt
1 cup sugar	3 teaspoons baking powder
2 cans flaked coconut	1 teaspoon allspice
2 eggs, beaten	½ teaspoon ginger
1½ cups flour	

Preheat the oven to 400° F.

Cream the butter and sugar thoroughly. Add the coconut and eggs; mix well. Sift the flour with the salt, baking powder, allspice and ginger; gradually stir into the coconut mixture.

Drop 1 teaspoon at a time onto a greased cookie sheet. Bake 8 to 10 minutes, or until well browned around the edges. Cool and store in an airtight container. *Makes 5 dozen.*

COCONUT CUPCAKES

3 cups shredded coconut	½ teaspoon baking powder
3 egg whites	⅛ teaspoon salt
⅔ cup sugar	¼ cup finely chopped pecans
⅓ cup cake flour	Candied cherries, halved

Preheat the oven to 325° F.

Chop the coconut, 1 cup at a time, in a blender until fine (or force through the fine blade of a food grinder); set aside. Beat the egg whites until foamy; gradually add the sugar and continue to beat until stiff peaks form. Fold in the coconut, sifted dry ingredients and nuts.

Using about 1 tablespoon of batter for each, spoon into 2-inch paper-lined foil baking cups and top each with a cherry half; bake 25 minutes, or until lightly browned. Store in an airtight container. *Makes 2 dozen.*

SAUCEPAN DATE BARS

1 cup margarine	½ teaspoon each nutmeg,
1½ cups sugar	cinnamon and cloves
2 eggs	¼ cup buttermilk
2¾ cups flour	2 cups chopped dates
½ teaspoon baking soda	1 cup chopped almonds
½ teaspoon salt	

Preheat the oven to 350° F.

Melt the margarine in a saucepan and remove from heat. Add the sugar and eggs and beat well. Mix the dry ingredients together, add with buttermilk to mixture in saucepan and mix well. Stir in the dates and almonds.

Spread in a greased 15 by 10 by 2-inch baking pan. Bake about 25 minutes. Cool and cut into 2-inch by 1-inch bars or into diamonds. *Makes about 75.*

MELT-IN-THE-MOUTH COOKIES

½ cup butter, softened
1 cup packed light brown
   sugar
1 teaspoon vanilla extract
1 egg

¾ cup flour
1 teaspoon baking powder
½ teaspoon salt
½ cup finely chopped nuts

Preheat the oven to 400° F.

Cream the butter. Add the sugar, vanilla and egg and beat until light. Mix together the flour, baking powder and salt. Add to the butter mixture and mix thoroughly, then stir in the nuts.

Drop by level teaspoonfuls onto ungreased cookie sheets. Bake 5 minutes. Remove from the oven and let set exactly 1 minute, then, with a broad spatula, pressing down firmly, quickly remove from cookie sheet. Cool on wire racks. Store in airtight containers. *Makes about 8 dozen.*

MOCHA BARS

1 cup butter or margarine,
   softened
1 cup packed brown sugar
2¼ cups flour
1 teaspoon dry instant
   coffee

½ teaspoon baking powder
¼ teaspoon salt
1 teaspoon almond extract
1 package (6 ounces) semisweet chocolate pieces
½ cup chopped almonds

Preheat the oven to 350° F.

In the large bowl of an electric mixer, cream the butter and sugar until fluffy. Stir together the flour, coffee, baking powder and salt; beat well into creamed mixture. Stir in the extract, chocolate and almonds. Press dough into a greased 15 by 10 by 1-inch pan and bake about 25 minutes. Cut into bars while warm. *Makes about 5 dozen cookies.*

MOCHA-NUT BUTTERBALLS

1 cup butter or margarine, softened
½ cup granulated sugar
2 teaspoons vanilla extract
2 teaspoons dry instant coffee
¼ cup unsweetened cocoa
1¾ cups flour
½ teaspoon salt
2 cups finely chopped pecans
Confectioners' sugar

Preheat the oven to 325° F.

Cream the butter, sugar and vanilla until light. Add the instant coffee, cocoa, flour and salt and mix well; add the nuts.

Shape into 1-inch balls and put on greased cookie sheets. Bake about 15 minutes, or until done. Cool on racks. Roll in confectioners' sugar. *Makes 6 dozen.*

NUT BARS

½ cup margarine, melted and cooled
½ cup light brown sugar, lightly packed
1 cup sifted flour

TOPPING

2 eggs
¼ teaspoon salt
1 cup light brown sugar,
   lightly packed
1 teaspoon vanilla extract

1 tablespoon all-purpose
   flour
1 cup finely chopped nuts
1 can (3½ ounces) flaked
   coconut

Preheat the oven to 350° F.

Combine the margarine and sugar and cream until fluffy. Stir in the flour until blended. Spread on the bottom of a well-greased 13 by 9 by 3-inch baking pan and bake 10 minutes.

While the cake is in the oven, prepare the topping by combining all the topping ingredients. Spread the topping on the partially baked cake and bake 20 minutes longer.

Cool on rack. Cut into 2 inch by 1-inch bars. Store in an airtight container in a cool place. *Makes about 3½ dozen.*

OATMEAL-RAISIN COOKIES

1 cup butter or margarine,
   softened
1½ cups sugar
1 cup seedless raisins

1½ cups flour
1 teaspoon baking soda
2½ cups quick-cooking rolled
   oats (not instant)

Preheat the oven to 375° F.

Cream the butter; gradually add the sugar and cream until light and fluffy. Stir in the raisins. Sift together the flour and baking soda and add to the first mixture with the oats. Mix well, using your hands. Shape into 1-inch balls, trying to cover the raisins.

Put 1 inch apart on lightly greased baking sheets. Bake 15 minutes, or until golden brown. Let cool slightly before removing to rack.

Store these cookies in an airtight container in a cool place. They also freeze well. *Makes about 8 dozen.*

ORNAMENTAL SUGAR COOKIES

Here are two recipes for light and dark sugar cookies that are firm enough to support heavy ornamental frosting. Use them to make cookies in special shapes for different occasions. If you wish to string them as Christmas-tree ornaments or as unusual decorations for a child's room, use a skewer or toothpick to make a hole in the top of each cookie after it has baked for 3 or 4 minutes, and put string or yarn through the hole after the cookie is cool and frosted.

We also include a recipe for an excellent ornamental frosting that can be tinted in various colors and used to make patterns and to color designs.

LIGHT ORNAMENTAL COOKIES

2 cups flour
1 cup sugar
¼ teaspoon salt
½ teaspoon baking powder
½ cup softened (not runny or whipped) butter

1 egg
2 tablespoons brandy, whiskey or rum (or 1 tablespoon each milk and lemon juice)
½ teaspoon vanilla extract

Sift the flour, sugar, salt and baking powder together. Add the butter and mix with your fingers until the mixture forms coarse crumbs. Add the egg and liquor. (Liquor produces a firmer, crisper cookie.) Add the vanilla and knead until the dough holds together. Form into a ball. Place in a bowl, cover and refrigerate until the dough is chilled enough to handle.

Preheat the oven to 400° F.

Divide the dough into thirds and roll out each third. For hanging ornaments, the dough should be ¼ inch thick; as a dessert cookie, roll it ⅛ inch thick. Cut with fancy cutters or by hand and place on lightly buttered cookie sheets. Allow space for the cookies to spread when baking. Bake 5 to 10 minutes, or until the cookies are done inside; break one open to see. Cool.

These cookies can be served plain or spread with Ornamental Frosting (see below) and decorated as you wish. *Makes about 6 dozen thin cookies.*

DARK ORNAMENTAL COOKIES

2½ cups flour
1 teaspoon cinnamon
½ teaspoon nutmeg
¼ teaspoon ground allspice
1 tablespoon ginger
½ teaspoon salt
¼ cup granulated sugar

⅓ cup dark unsulfured molasses
½ cup butter (not whipped)
⅓ cup packed brown sugar
½ teaspoon baking soda
1 egg

Sift the flour, spices, salt and granulated sugar together and set aside. Heat the molasses to the boiling point and remove from heat. Add the butter and brown sugar and stir until the butter melts. Add the baking soda and stir well. Pour over the flour-spice mixture, stirring well. Add the egg and knead until dough holds together. Chill slightly.

Preheat the oven to 350° F.

Roll small amounts of the dough on a floured board with a floured rolling pin. If you aren't an experienced cook, roll between sheets of floured waxed paper. Dough should be rolled about ¼ inch thick if it is to be used for hanging ornaments. If for other purposes, roll ⅛ thick. Cut with floured cutters. Place cookies 2 inches apart on floured pans and bake 8 to 10 minutes, or until cookies are done inside; break one open to see. Remove cookies from pan as soon as baked.

Decorate with Ornamental Frosting when cold. *Makes about 6 dozen thin, 2-inch cookies.*

ORNAMENTAL FROSTING

This wonderful frosting gets unusually hard and glossy. It is durable and adhesive and isn't apt to crack. If you make it ahead and put it in tightly covered jars in the refrigerator, it will stay soft for several days. It is best to make small amounts at a time, using an electric mixer.

About 1 cup confectioners'   ½ teaspoon cream of tartar
        sugar   Food coloring
  1 egg white

Beat the confectioners' sugar and the egg white together thoroughly. If the icing seems too runny, add a little more sugar; it should be of the right consistency to flow easily through an icing tube or paper cone. Just before taking from the mixer, add the cream of tartar and beat again. Add different food colorings to several parts of the batch for decorative purposes.

PFEFFERNUSSE

These cookies from Germany keep well and are excellent for Christmas mailing.

  3 cups sifted flour   ¼ teaspoon black pepper
  ¾ teaspoon salt   ¾ teaspoon baking soda
  ¾ teaspoon baking powder   ⅛ teaspoon ground aniseed
  ¾ teaspoon allspice   1 cup honey
  ¾ teaspoon mace   3 tablespoons shortening
  ¾ teaspoon cardamom   1 egg

FROSTING
  1 egg white   1½ cups sifted confectioners'
  2 teaspoons honey   sugar
  ¼ teaspoon ground aniseed

Sift together the flour, salt, baking powder, allspice, mace, cardamom, pepper, baking soda and aniseed and set aside. Heat the honey, but do not let it boil; add the shortening and cool. Beat in the egg. Stir in the sifted dry ingredients until just blended. Let the dough stand 10 minutes to stiffen enough to handle easily.

While the dough is standing, preheat the oven to 350° F.

Shape the dough into 1-inch balls. Place on lightly greased cookie sheets. Bake 13 to 15 minutes. Cool.

While the cookies are baking, prepare the *Frosting:* Combine the egg white, honey and aniseed, then gradually add the confectioners' sugar, beating until smooth.

Put 12 to 14 cooled cookies in a bowl, add 2 tablespoons of the frosting and stir to frost all sides of the cookies. Lift out with a fork onto a rack. Repeat until they are all frosted.

Store these cookies in an airtight container for a week before giving. *Makes 60.*

SCOTCH SHORTBREAD

6 cups sifted flour   2 egg yolks
1 cup sugar
1 pound soft butter or
    margarine

Preheat the oven to 350° F.

Mix the flour, sugar and butter thoroughly with your hands. Add the egg yolks, one at a time, kneading the dough well after each addition. Divide into 8 parts and roll each part into a circle about ½ inch thick. Prick with a fork.

Bake at 350° F. for 15 minutes, then bake at 300° F. for 30 minutes. Cut each into eighths; return to the oven to brown the edges. *Makes 64.*

SESAME-ANISE COOKIES

The dough for these Mexican cookies should be prepared the day before and chilled overnight.

1 tablespoon aniseed
2 tablespoons boiling water
¾ cup butter
⅔ cup sugar
⅛ teaspoon baking soda

2 eggs
2 cups sifted flour
3 tablespoons sesame seed, toasted

Combine the aniseed and boiling water and steep while mixing the dough. Cream the butter with the sugar and baking soda. Beat in 1 egg. Drain the aniseed and add. Stir in the flour, a little at a time. Mix well. Chill dough overnight.

The next day, preheat the oven to 400° F.

Roll the dough into ½-inch balls. Place on ungreased cookie sheets 1½ inches apart. Put a piece of waxed paper over the cookies and flatten to 1/16-inch thickness with bottom of a glass. Remove waxed paper. Beat the remaining egg and brush it over the tops of the cookies. Sprinkle with sesame seed. Bake 7 or 8 minutes. *Makes 12 dozen.*

SESAME-OAT COOKIES

½ cup butter, softened
1 cup packed light brown sugar
1 egg
3 tablespoons milk
¾ cup sesame seed
1¼ cups quick-cooking rolled oats (not instant)

¾ cup dark unsulfured seedless raisins
1¼ cups all-purpose flour
½ teaspoon salt
½ teaspoon baking soda
½ teaspoon cinnamon

Preheat the oven to 375° F.

Cream the butter and sugar together. Beat in the egg and milk. Stir in the sesame seed, oats and raisins. Mix together the flour, salt, baking soda and cinnamon; add to the first mixture and combine well. Drop by rounded teaspoonfuls onto ungreased cookie sheets. Flatten slightly. (These cookies do not spread.) Bake 10 to 12 minutes, or until golden brown. Cool on racks. *Makes about 4 dozen.*

THIMBLE COOKIES

1 cup butter or margarine, softened	4 egg yolks
½ cup granulated or confectioners' sugar	1 teaspoon vanilla extract
	2 cups all-purpose flour
	Jam or jelly

Preheat the oven to 325° F.

Cream the butter and sugar. Add the egg yolks and vanilla and beat until light and fluffy. Stir in the flour and, if necessary, chill until firm enough to handle.

With floured hands, roll into 1-inch balls. Put 1½ inches apart on cookie sheets. Using a lightly floured thimble, make a small indentation in the center of each cookie. Fill with jam. Bake about 25 minutes. Cool on racks. *Makes about 4 dozen.*

Pies
and
Tarts

PIE IS the all-time American favorite. These recipes are for gift pies that keep well and travel easily. A few of them require refrigeration, and we've indicated when this is so.

Five basic pie crusts are given: standard pastry, crumb shell, cookie shell, cream-cheese pastry and boiling-water pastry. Try them all and use whichever you prefer in these recipes, though crumb shells cannot be used in place of unbaked pastry shells.

Be sure that you have the right equipment for pie-baking. You will need a mixing bowl, measuring cups and spoons, a board or pastry cloth, a rolling pin, a pastry blender and pie pans in several sizes. A 9-inch pie pan is the most convenient size to have; it will serve six to eight people. A pastry cloth and a cover for the rolling pin are also very useful.

For a well-browned bottom crust, bake pies on the lowest rack of a thoroughly preheated oven. Pastry browns best in either dull aluminum or glass pie pans. If you use a foil pan, put it on a baking sheet so that the bottom browns evenly.

Most pies should be prepared no more than a day before you plan to give them, unless you wish to freeze them. Fruit pies freeze well, but bake them before you freeze them so that the bottom crust does not get soggy. Freeze them fast, unwrapped, and then wrap and store them. To defrost a baked pie, unwrap it and leave it at room temperature for several hours or defrost it partially and then heat it in a 350° F. oven until it is warm.

Unfilled pie shells can be frozen, baked or unbaked, but

baked shells will keep longer, about 4 to 6 months. Thaw baked shells unwrapped at room temperature or in a 350° F. oven. Unbaked shells should go right into the oven while they are still frozen.

You can keep pie dough in a ball in the refrigerator for about a week, or you can freeze it.

Tips on Baking Pies

• Handle the dough as little as possible if you wish the crust to be light and flaky.
• If you chill the dough before rolling it, it will be easier to handle. Let it warm up for a half hour or so before you roll it.
• When rolling the dough, use as little extra flour as possible.
• Start rolling the dough from the center. Lift the rolling pin and repeat until the dough is about ⅛ inch thick.
• Use a little more than half the dough for the bottom crust. Roll it 2 inches larger than the pan.
• Pat the bottom crust loosely but firmly into the pie pan.
• Prick the top crust with a fork to allow steam to escape. Flute the edges or press them down with a fork.

If you prefer, use a woven, latticework crust on the top.
• When baking an unfilled pie shell, prick it all over with a fork or fill it with dry beans or rice to keep it from bubbling up while baking.

Ideas for Giving Pies

You can bake pies in foil pans and wrap them in colored foil, tied with a ribbon. Or, if you feel especially generous, bake and give a pie in a pottery or china pie plate or a new glass pie dish. You can also give a pie on a pretty platter or tray, or in an antique pie box, if you are lucky enough to find one. Or present them on a cake pedestal or a lazy Susan, or in a shallow basket. Accompany your gift with a slender French rolling pin, if you wish, and include the recipe, giving suggestions as to whether the pie should be served warm or cold.

STANDARD PASTRY

2 cups sifted flour
1 teaspoon salt
⅔ cup hydrogenated shorten-
    ing or ½ cup lard

4 to 5 tablespoons cold water

Mix the flour and the salt. Cut in the shortening, using a pastry blender or your fingers. Add the cold water, a few drops at a time, mixing with a fork and using only enough water to get the dough into a ball. *Makes enough for one 2-crust 8-inch or 9-inch pie, or for two pie shells.*

CRUMB SHELL

1¼ cups fine graham-cracker,
    vanilla-wafer, corn-flake
    or ginger-snap crumbs

¼ cup soft butter
2 to 4 tablespoons sugar
1 egg (optional)

Mix the crumbs and the butter. Add sugar to taste, depending on the sweetness of the crumbs you're using. If you wish a firm graham-cracker crust that cuts without crumbling, add the egg and flute the edges. Press the crumbs into a 9-inch pie pan. Bake 8 minutes in a preheated 375° F. oven (10 minutes in a 350° F. oven if you've added the egg). *Makes one 9-inch pie shell.*

COOKIE SHELL

1 cup unsifted flour
½ teaspoon salt
1 tablespoon sugar
6 tablespoons butter or
  margarine

1 egg yolk
1 tablespoon water
4½ teaspoons lemon juice or
  rum

Mix together the flour, salt and sugar. Blend in the butter. In a separate bowl, beat the egg yolk, water and lemon juice together; add to the first mixture and blend in with a fork. Shape into a ball and chill. Roll out to ¼ inch thick and fit in a pie pan or layer pan. *Makes one 9-inch pie shell.*

CREAM-CHEESE PASTRY

2 cups sifted flour
¾ teaspoon salt
⅔ cup hydrogenated
  shortening

12 ounces cream cheese

Mix the flour and salt. Work in the shortening and the cream cheese. *Makes enough for one 2-crust 8-inch or 9-inch pie or for two pie shells.*

BOILING-WATER PASTRY

⅔ cup hydrogenated
  shortening
⅓ cup boiling water

2 cups sifted flour
1 teaspoon salt

Put the shortening in a bowl and gradually add the boiling water, creaming with a fork until well mixed. Add the flour and the salt, mixing thoroughly with a fork. *Makes enough for one 2-crust 8-inch or 9-inch pie or for two pie shells.*

APPLE-MINCE PIE

2 cups prepared mincemeat
4 tart apples, peeled, cored and sliced (about 6 cups)
½ cup cognac or brandy
½ cup chopped walnuts
2 tablespoons flour
1 teaspoon grated lemon rind

2 tablespoons lemon juice
Pastry for 2-crust 9-inch pie
2 tablespoons butter or margarine
1 egg beaten with 1 tablespoon water

Preheat the oven to 400° F.

Combine the mincemeat, apples, cognac, walnuts, flour and lemon rind and juice. Spoon into a pastry-lined 9-inch pie pan and dot with butter. Make lattice top, flute rim and brush with egg mixture. Bake on lowest rack in oven about 45 minutes, or until golden brown. *Note:* After about 30 minutes, put a foil collar around the edge of the crust to prevent excessive browning. Cool on a wire rack.

APPLE PIE WITH CHEDDAR-CHEESE PASTRY

CHEDDAR-CHEESE PASTRY

2¼ cups flour
1 teaspoon salt
¾ cup shortening

½ cup finely shredded Cheddar cheese
5 tablespoons water

APPLE FILLING

5 cups peeled, cored and
sliced tart apples
½ cup granulated sugar
¼ cup packed light brown
sugar
2 tablespoons flour
½ teaspoon grated lemon
rind

2 tablespoons lemon juice
¼ teaspoon salt
⅛ teaspoon nutmeg
1 tablespoon butter or
margarine
1 egg beaten with 1 tablespoon water

Prepare the *Cheddar-Cheese Pastry:* Stir the flour and salt to-gether. Cut in the shortening with a pastry blender or your fingers; add the cheese and mix lightly with a fork. Sprinkle with the water, a tablespoon at a time, and mix lightly with a fork until just moistened. Form into a large ball, wrap in plas-tic wrap and refrigerate for at least ½ hour.

Preheat the oven to 400° F.

Roll out the pastry into 2 circles to line and cover a 9-inch pie pan.

Apple Filling: combine the apples, sugars, flour, lemon rind and juice, salt and nutmeg. Turn into a pastry-lined pie pan, dot with butter, adjust top crust, seal and flute edges. Brush with the egg mixture and bake on lowest rack in the oven for about 1 hour, or until golden brown. *Note:* After 30 minutes, put a foil collar around the edge of the crust to prevent exces-sive browning. Cool on a wire rack.

APRICOT-PRUNE PIE

2½ cups cooked dried apricots and pitted prunes
Pastry for 2-crust 9-inch
pie
½ cup cooking liquid from
fruit
1 tablespoon cornstarch

½ cup sugar
⅓ teaspoon salt
¼ teaspoon each cinnamon
and nutmeg
Juice 1 lemon
1 tablespoon butter or
margarine

Preheat the oven to 425° F.

Put the fruit in the bottom crust. Mix the cooking liquid, cornstarch, sugar, salt, and spices. Cook until slightly thickened. Stir in the lemon juice and butter; pour over fruit. Moisten the edges of the pastry, and cover with the top crust which has been slit to allow steam to escape. Press edges together with tines of fork. Bake about 45 minutes.

This pie can be frozen until ready to give. Suggest serving warm or cold.

CHESS PIE

2 eggs
1½ tablespoons all-purpose
    flour
⅔ cup packed brown sugar
½ teaspoon salt
1 teaspoon vanilla extract

1 cup heavy cream
½ cup seedless raisins
1 cup cut-up pitted dates
1 cup broken walnut meats
    Unbaked 9-inch pie shell

Preheat the oven to 350° F.

Beat the eggs until thick and lemon-colored. Mix the flour, sugar and salt, add to the eggs and beat well. Stir in the vanilla, cream, raisins, dates and walnuts. Spoon into the pie shell. Bake for 50 minutes or until a knife inserted in the center comes out clean. Refrigerate until ready to give, no more than a day or so.

CHOCOLATE BROWNIE PIE

1 can (14 ounces) sweet-
    ened condensed milk
¼ teaspoon salt
1 package (6 ounces) semi-
    sweet chocolate pieces
1 teaspoon vanilla extract

2 tablespoons flour
2 eggs, separated
½ cup coarsely chopped nuts
2 tablespoons sugar
    Unbaked 9-inch pastry
    shell

Preheat the oven to 350° F.

Heat the milk and salt to boiling, stirring. Remove from heat; beat in the chocolate, vanilla and flour. Add egg yolks one at a time, beating thoroughly after each addition. Stir in the nuts. Beat the egg whites until stiff, but not dry. Gradually beat in the sugar, continuing to beat until very stiff and glossy. Fold into the chocolate mixture. Pour into the pastry shell, and bake for 40 minutes, or until firm.

You can keep this pie in the refrigerator for a day or so before giving it. It can also be frozen.

COTTAGE-CHEESE PIE

1½ cups creamed cottage
    cheese
1 tablespoon flour
⅛ teaspoon salt
1 cup heavy cream
⅔ cup granulated sugar
    Grated rind of 1 lemon
    Juice of 1 lemon

3 eggs, separated
⅓ cup dried currants
    Unbaked 9-inch pastry
    shell
    Confectioners' sugar

Preheat the oven to 450° F.

Force the cheese through a fine sieve or food mill. Blend in the flour and salt. Then stir in the cream, granulated sugar, lemon rind and juice. Beat the egg whites until stiff, but not dry; then beat yolks until thick and lemon-colored. Stir the yolks and currants into the cheese mixture. Fold in whites, and pour into the pastry shell.

Bake at 450° F. for 10 minutes, then reduce heat to 350° F. and bake 45 minutes longer, or until the pie is firm. Cool, sprinkle with confectioners' sugar and refrigerate until ready to give, no more than a day or so. This pie can be frozen.

LEMON PIE

2 cups sugar
1 tablespoon flour
1 tablespoon cornmeal
4 eggs
¼ cup butter, softened
¼ cup light cream

2 tablespoons grated lemon rind
¼ cup lemon juice
Unbaked 9-inch pie shell
Whipped cream

Preheat the oven to 375° F.

Combine the sugar, flour and cornmeal in a large bowl and toss lightly with a fork to mix. Add the eggs, butter, cream, lemon rind and juice; beat with a rotary or electric beater until smooth and thoroughly blended, then pour into the pie shell. Bake on lowest rack in the oven for 45 minutes, or until golden brown. Cool. Top with whipped cream.

MINCEMEAT PIE

1 jar (32 ounces) prepared mincemeat
Grated rind of 1 lemon

Pastry for 2-crust 9-inch pie
1 egg yolk beaten with 2 teaspoons milk or cream

Preheat the oven to 425° F.

Combine the mincemeat and lemon rind and set aside. Roll out two-thirds of the pastry and line a 9-inch pie pan. Trim the edges and flute in a pretty pattern. Pour in mincemeat. Roll out remaining pastry to ⅛-inch thickness and cut out ten ¾-inch-wide strips; arrange 6 strips crosswise and 4 strips lengthwise, lattice fashion, on pie. Trim ends of strips and press into sides of shell. Brush the pastry with the egg yolk-and-milk mixture. Bake in 425° F. oven for 10 minutes; reduce heat to 350° F. and bake 25 to 30 minutes, or until done.

This pie can be kept in the refrigerator, tightly covered, for up to a week before giving. Suggest sprinkling it with a few tablespoons of light rum and some chopped pistachio nuts before reheating it in a preheated 325° F. oven.

EARLY AMERICAN PEAR PIE

¾ cup sugar
2 tablespoons flour
½ teaspoon each nutmeg and cinnamon
6 cups thinly sliced, peeled, ripe pears

Pastry for 2-crust 9-inch pie
2 tablespoons butter

Preheat the oven to 425° F.

Mix the sugar, flour, nutmeg and cinnamon. Add the pears and mix lightly. Line the pie pan with half the pastry. Add the filling, dot with butter, and adjust, flute and prick the top crust. Bake for about 50 minutes. You can freeze this pie, if you wish, until ready to give. Suggest serving it warm, reheated in a preheated 325° F. oven.

CHOCOLATE PECAN PIE

¾ cup dark corn syrup
3 eggs
½ teaspoon salt
1½ teaspoons vanilla extract

1½ cups semisweet chocolate pieces, melted
¾ cup pecan halves
Unbaked 9-inch pie shell

Preheat the oven to 350° F.

In a large bowl, combine the syrup, eggs, salt and vanilla and beat well with a wooden spoon. Slowly add the chocolate to the egg mixture and beat briskly until blended; stir in the pecans and then pour into the pie shell. Bake about 30 minutes. Cool.

HONEY-PUMPKIN PIE

1½ cups canned pumpkin
½ cup honey
2 teaspoons grated orange
    rind
½ teaspoon each cinnamon
    and salt
½ teaspoon vanilla extract

¼ teaspoon each nutmeg
    and ginger
2 eggs, beaten
1 cup evaporated milk
    Unbaked 9-inch pie shell
1 egg white, slightly beaten

Preheat the oven to 425° F.

In a large bowl, combine all ingredients, except last 2. Beat until well blended. Brush the pie shell with the egg white and bake for 5 minutes. Remove from the oven, pour in the filling and bake 45 minutes, or until firm. Serve warm or cool.

SOUR-CREAM PUMPKIN PIE

1½ cups cooked or canned
    pumpkin
1½ cups sour cream
¾ teaspoon cinnamon
¼ teaspoon nutmeg
¼ teaspoon ginger

¼ teaspoon salt
½ cup packed brown sugar
½ cup granulated sugar
3 eggs, separated
    Unbaked 9-inch pie shell

Mix the pumpkin, sour cream, seasonings and sugars in the top part of a double boiler. Stir over hot water until heated through. Beat the egg yolks until light and fluffy. Stir into a small amount of the hot mixture, then add this egg yolk mixture to the remaining hot mixture. Cook over hot water, stirring, until very thick; set aside to cool.

Preheat the oven to 425° F.

Brush the pie shell with a small amount of the egg whites.

Prick the shell well and bake it for 10 minutes. Beat the remaining egg whites until stiff but not dry. Carefully fold into the pumpkin mixture, then pile into the shell. Bake at 425° F. for 10 minutes, then at 350° F. for 40 minutes more. Cool.

TART PASTRY

2 cups sifted flour
½ teaspoon baking powder
¼ cup sugar
½ teaspoon salt

⅔ cup soft shortening
1 egg, beaten with 2 tablespoons milk

Sift together the flour, baking powder, sugar and salt. Cut in the shortening. Using a fork, lightly mix in the egg and milk. Form into a ball and chill.

Preheat the oven to 425° F.

Divide the dough into 12 parts. Roll each piece to form a circle 4½ inches in diameter. Fit over the backs of 3½-inch tart pans or trim edges with a pastry wheel and fit inside 3½-inch foil pans. Bake for 10 minutes. Cool and remove from pans. *Makes 12 baked tart shells.*

Use to make Peach Cream Tarts (below), Glazed Cherry Tarts (p. 127), or Double-Chocolate Tarts (p. 128).

PEACH CREAM TARTS

3 cups milk
¾ cup sugar
6 tablespoons cornstarch
½ teaspoon salt
3 eggs, beaten
1 tablespoon butter

2 teaspoons vanilla extract
12 baked tart shells (See Tart
Pastry, above)
6 ripe peaches
Chopped nuts

Scald the milk in the top of a double boiler over boiling water. Mix the sugar, cornstarch and salt; stir into the milk. Cook, stirring, until thick. Cover and cook 10 minutes longer. Add a small amount to the eggs, then add the eggs to the mixture in the double boiler and cook for 5 minutes. Add the butter and vanilla. Chill.

Fill the tart shells with the vanilla filling and top each with half a peach, thinly sliced. Sprinkle with chopped nuts and keep refrigerated until ready to give. These tarts should be filled shortly before giving and moved quickly from one refrigerator to another. *Makes 12 tarts.*

GLAZED CHERRY TARTS

FILLING

3 cups milk
¾ cup sugar
6 tablespoons cornstarch
½ teaspoon salt

3 eggs, beaten
1 tablespoon butter
1 teaspoon vanilla extract
½ teaspoon almond extract

CHERRY TOPPING

1 pound (or one 1-pound can) pitted red sour cherries
¾ cup apple juice or juice from canned cherries
¼ cup sugar

2 tablespoons cornstarch
⅛ teaspoon salt
1 tablespoon lemon juice
Red food coloring
12 baked tart shells (See Tart Pastry, p. 126)

First, prepare the *Filling:* Scald the milk in the top of a double boiler over boiling water. Mix the sugar, cornstarch and salt; stir into the milk. Cook, stirring, until thick. Cover and cook 10 minutes longer. Add a small amount to the eggs, then add the eggs to the mixture in the double boiler and cook for 5 minutes. Add the butter, and vanilla and almond flavorings. Chill.

Next, prepare the *Cherry Topping:* Simmer the cherries in the apple juice until soft, or, if you are using canned cherries, drain them, reserving ¾ cup of juice. Mix the sugar, cornstarch and salt in a saucepan. Add the apple or cherry juice and cook, stirring, until thickened. Add the cherries and lemon juice. Add the food coloring. Cool.

Shortly before giving, fill the tart shells with the Filling and top each shell with the Cherry Topping. Keep refrigerated. *Makes 12 tarts.*

DOUBLE-CHOCOLATE TARTS

3 squares unsweetened
  chocolate
3 cups milk
6 tablespoons sugar
6 tablespoons cornstarch
½ teaspoon salt

3 eggs, beaten
1 tablespoon butter
2 teaspoons vanilla extract
12 baked tart shells (See Tart
  Pastry, p. 126)
Chocolate sauce

Melt the chocolate in the milk in the top of a double boiler over boiling water; beat until smooth. Mix the sugar, cornstarch and salt; stir into the milk. Cook, stirring, until thick. Cover and cook 10 minutes longer. Add a small amount to the eggs, then add the eggs to the mixture in the double boiler and cook for 5 minutes. Add the butter and vanilla. Chill.

Shortly before giving, fill the tart shells with the chocolate filling and dribble chocolate sauce over each tart. Keep refrigerated. *Makes 12 tarts.*

Desserts
and
Sweet
Sauces

PUDDING-TYPE DESSERTS and sweet dessert sauces are easy to make at home, but are often overlooked as gift possibilities. Give a dessert and a sauce to serve with it, or give two or three different sauces in separate containers.

Some of these desserts and sauces must be kept refrigerated; give them when you do not have far to travel. Others must be reheated before serving: include a gift card with hand-written instructions for heating (you'll find *our* suggestions with the recipe), and don't forget to suggest appropriate things to serve with the sauce.

These delicious dessert sauces will work wonders with leftover or uninteresting store-bought cake. They complement a variety of desserts: ice cream or sherbet; plain chocolate or white cake; cheesecake, pound cake or gingerbread; vanilla, lemon, rice or bread pudding; gelatin desserts; berries, melons or other fruit; pies, tarts, pancakes and waffles. Use highly flavored sauces with bland desserts; mild sauces with spicy or strongly flavored desserts.

Ideas for Giving Desserts and Sweet Sauces

Give desserts in a pretty glass or ceramic jar, a copper mold, a soufflé dish or a glass or foil baking dish. Transparent containers are nice when the dessert is especially pretty: use a small glass fish bowl, for example, to present lovely alternating layers of Dried Fruit Compote (p. 133) and Plain Custard Sauce (p. 141).

Save nicely shaped vinegar and wine bottles to use for dessert sauces. Pretty glass bottles with stoppers can be found in gift stores; old ones in antique stores. Try giving several sauces, matching the bottles and contrasting the colors.

Desserts can also be packaged in individual portions: use custard cups, tiny soufflé dishes or inexpensive clear plastic drinking cups. Wrap each portion separately, using blue and bright green tissue paper and tying with blue and green ribbon; present them all in a little basket or a colored paper shopping bag, if you wish.

DATE-GRAHAM PUDDING

½ cup sugar	½ cup cold water
½ cup graham (whole-wheat) flour	2 cups boiling water
1 teaspoon salt	¾ cup diced, pitted dates

Mix the sugar, flour and salt in the top of a double boiler and add the ½ cup of cold water. Gradually stir in the 2 cups of boiling water and cook over direct heat, stirring, for 10 minutes. Add the dates. Cover and cook over simmering water for 1¼ hours. Cool and chill. *Makes 4 servings.*

You can give this dessert in a small bowl or in individual plastic cups. Accompany it with Walnut Sauce (p. 148), or suggest serving it with whipped cream.

DRIED FRUIT COMPOTE

1 pound mixed dried fruit
2 pieces of lemon rind
½ cup toasted, slivered almonds, or other nuts, chopped

Cover the fruit and lemon rind with water in a small saucepan and slowly bring to a boil. Simmer, covered, until the fruit is soft but still holds its shape. Chill in the liquid.

Give cold, sprinkled with almonds, in a glass jar. If you wish, you can make Brandy Custard Sauce (p. 142) and combine layers of the fruit compote with layers of the custard sauce in a glass bowl, saving the almonds for the very top. It makes a most attractive gift, but must be moved quickly from refrigerator to refrigerator, so it should be saved for when you do not have far to travel.

SPICY FRUIT

3 cups mixed dried fruit, such as pitted prunes, pitted dates, apricots and figs
½ cup golden raisins
⅓ cup sugar
3-inch cinnamon stick
6 whole cloves
¼ teaspoon salt
6 cups water
1 can (6 ounces) frozen orange-juice concentrate

Cut the mixed fruit into small pieces. Combine with the raisins, sugar, cinnamon stick, cloves and salt; add the 6 cups of water. Bring to a boil and simmer for 15 minutes. Add the orange juice and mix well. Remove the cinnamon stick and cloves. *Makes 2 quarts.*

Give the chilled fruit in a 2-quart glass or ceramic jar. Label it and suggest that it be served alone or with ice cream or vanilla pudding.

GREEK KATAIFE

5 cups crushed shredded- wheat biscuits	2 cups chopped walnuts
¾ cup melted butter	1½ teaspoons cinnamon
	Honey Syrup

Preheat the oven to 300° F.

Mix the shredded-wheat biscuits, butter, walnuts and cinnamon and put the mixture in a greased 9-inch square pan. Bake about 45 minutes. *Makes 9 servings.*

Pack in gift containers and refrigerate until ready to give. Give with Honey Syrup (p. 142), which should be heated and poured over the *kataife* before serving.

STEAMED MINCEMEAT ·PUDDING

1 cup sugar	2 teaspoons baking powder
½ cup butter or margarine, softened	½ teaspoon salt
	½ teaspoon cinnamon
2 eggs	⅔ cup evaporated milk
1¾ cups flour	1½ cups prepared mincemeat

In the large bowl of an electric mixer, cream the sugar and butter until fluffy; add the eggs one at a time, beating well after each. Stir together the flour, baking powder, salt and cinnamon; add to the creamed mixture alternately with the evaporated milk and beat until smooth. Stir in the mincemeat.

Pour the mixture into a greased 1½-quart pudding mold;

grease the inside of the lid and cover the mold. Or, if you wish to make individual puddings, spoon the mixture into 8 greased 6-ounce custard cups to about 1 inch from the top; cover each with a square of foil and secure the foil with an elastic band.

Put the mold or custard cups on a rack in a large pot, or use 2 pots, if necessary. Add enough boiling water to come halfway up the sides of the mold or the custard cups. Cover and steam: 1½ hours for the mold, or a little longer if the mold has no tube; 1 hour for the custard cups. Remove and put on a rack until cool enough to handle. Unmold. *Makes 8 servings.*

Wrap the pudding or each individual pudding in plastic and tie with gold or silver cord. Arrange the small puddings in a colorful shopping bag or a small basket, if you wish. Give Mincemeat Pudding with a jar of Orange-Honey Hard Sauce (p. 145), and instructions to serve the pudding warm (reheated in the top of a double boiler or in a slow oven), sprinkled with confectioners' sugar, if desired, and accompanied with the hard sauce.

BRANDIED PEACHES

3 cups sugar	Ascorbic acid tablets
2 cups water	(optional)
5 pounds small peaches	1 cup brandy

Bring the sugar and water to a boil, stirring down the crystals from the sides of the pan.

In a separate pot, cover the peaches with boiling water and let them stand 1 minute; cool quickly under running water. Peel and put in a pan of slightly salted water to prevent browning, or dissolve ascorbic acid tablets in the water according to package directions. Do not let them stand more than 15 to 20 minutes.

Add 8 to 10 peaches at a time to the sugar syrup; simmer 10 minutes or until tender. Remove and repeat the process until all the peaches have been cooked.

Add the brandy to the syrup and bring it to a boil for about a minute. Pour over the peaches. *Makes about 5 pints.*

These peaches will keep for some time under refrigeration. Package them in attractive jars, ready for giving. If you wish to keep them for a very long time, pack them in hot, sterilized jars and pour the boiling syrup over them, following the directions for Jellies and Jams (p. 173–75).

PRUNES IN CLARET

1 pound dried prunes	½ cup water
2 cups claret wine	⅓ cup sugar

Wash the prunes and put them in a deep bowl. Cover them with the 2 cups of wine and ½ cup of water. Let them stand, covered, in the refrigerator overnight. On the next day, simmer them in the same liquid until tender. Add the sugar and simmer a few minutes more. Cool and refrigerate until ready to give.

ENGLISH PLUM PUDDING

½ cup chopped dates	½ cup chopped nuts
¾ cup dark seedless raisins	½ cup fine, dry breadcrumbs
¾ cup golden raisins	1 cup (¼ pound) minced suet
¼ cup chopped candied citron	1 cup sifted flour
¼ cup chopped, mixed, candied fruit	1 teaspoon salt
¼ cup chopped candied orange peel	1½ teaspoons baking powder
1½ cups beer	¾ teaspoon soda
4 eggs	1 teaspoon cinnamon
1½ cups brown sugar, packed	⅛ teaspoon cloves
	⅛ teaspoon allspice

Combine the fruits and peel in a bowl; add the beer and let stand at least 1 hour.

Beat the eggs with the brown sugar and add to the fruit-beer mixture. Stir in the nuts, crumbs and suet. Sift the dry ingredients and spices; stir into the fruit mixture.

Turn into 4 well-greased pint or two 1-quart pudding molds, filling ¾ full. Cover tightly with aluminum foil; tie securely. Put on a rack in a deep kettle; pour in boiling water to half the depth of the molds. Cover; steam 2½ hours, adding more water if necessary. Remove from steamer; immediately remove foil covers. Cool completely. Re-cover and store in the refrigerator.

Give each pudding in its mold with instructions to re-cover and steam about ¾ of an hour before serving to heat through and to unmold the pudding before serving it. Accompany your gift of plum pudding with a container of Brandy Hard Sauce (p. 144), or suggest pouring heated, flaming brandy over the pudding after it is brought to the table.

CUSTARD RICE PUDDING

½ cup cooked rice	1½ teaspoons grated lemon
3 eggs, beaten	rind
½ cup sugar	½ cup raisins
¼ teaspoon salt	3½ cups milk
1 teaspoon vanilla	Nutmeg

Preheat the oven to 300° F.

Mix the rice, eggs, sugar, salt, vanilla, lemon rind, raisins and milk. Pour into a shallow baking dish and sprinkle with nutmeg. Set in a pan of hot water and bake about 1½ hours. *Makes 6 servings*.

Keep this pudding in the refrigerator and give it within a day or so of making it. It can be served cold and is good plain or with a number of dessert sauces.

RUSSIAN APRICOT SAUCE

8 ounces (1½ cups) dried apricots	⅓ cup sugar ½ to ⅔ cup muscatel wine

Put the apricots in a saucepan, add 1¼ cups of water, bring to a boil and simmer until very tender, adding more water if necessary. Force through a sieve or food mill and put back in the saucepan. Add the sugar and ½ cup of hot water. Bring to a boil, stirring. Add the muscatel and simmer for a minute or two. *Makes 2 cups.*

This sauce keeps well under refrigeration. Spoon it into an attractive glass jar or jars and give with Ginger Pound Cake (p. 83) or any plain cake or pudding. It is good warm or cold and is fine with ice cream or sherbet.

HOT BANANA-FUDGE TOPPING

4 squares unsweetened chocolate	⅛ teaspoon salt
1 cup sugar	½ teaspoon vanilla extract
¾ cup undiluted evaporated milk	2 ripe bananas, sliced

Melt the chocolate over boiling water. Stir in the sugar, cover and cook ½ hour, stirring once or twice. Add the evaporated milk, salt and vanilla and beat vigorously with a spoon until smooth and thick. Add the bananas and heat, stirring in well, for another 5 to 10 minutes. *Makes about 2 cups.*

This sauce keeps well in the refrigerator. Spoon it into the container in which you plan to give it—an earthenware crock would be nice—and give it with instructions to reheat in a double boiler before serving with ice cream, plain cake or pudding.

BUTTERSCOTCH SAUCE

2 cups packed light brown
   sugar
½ cup undiluted evaporated
   milk

¼ teaspoon salt
⅓ cup light corn syrup
⅓ cup butter or margarine

Combine the sugar, milk, salt, corn syrup and butter in a saucepan. Bring to a boil and cook rapidly for 3 minutes, or to 220° F. on a candy thermometer. *Makes 2 cups.*
   Pack in gift containers and suggest serving hot or cold.

FRENCH CARAMEL SAUCE

2 cups granulated sugar   ½ cup water

Put the sugar in a heavy skillet, preferably an iron one. Cook it over high heat, stirring *constantly* with a wooden spoon, scraping the sugar from the bottom of the pan until it forms coarse crumbs or lumps. When it begins to melt, lower the heat and continue stirring, scraping particles from the bottom and sides of the pan until the syrup is clear and caramel-brown, like maple syrup. Add the ½ cup of water at once. The mixture will lump once more. Continue cooking and stirring over low heat until it again reaches the consistency of maple syrup. Do not cook too long, for it thickens as it stands.
   Pack the mixture into gift containers. *Makes 1¾ cups.*

CHOCOLATE FUDGE SAUCE

1 cup milk	2 cups sugar
4 squares unsweetened	¼ cup light corn syrup
chocolate	2 tablespoons butter
¼ teaspoon salt	1 teaspoon vanilla extract

Heat the milk and chocolate together over low heat, stirring constantly. Beat until smooth. Add the salt, sugar and corn syrup. Bring to a boil and cook, stirring, 5 minutes. Remove from heat and stir in the butter and vanilla. *Makes 2 cups.*

Pack in gift containers and refrigerate until ready to give. Suggest serving warm or cold on ice cream, cream puffs, plain cake or pudding.

CHOCOLATE-NUT CRACKLE SAUCE

¼ cup margarine	1 package (6 ounces) semi-
1 cup medium-fine chopped	sweet chocolate pieces
walnuts	

Melt the margarine in a heavy skillet over moderate heat. Add the walnuts and cook, stirring to prevent burning, until light golden brown. Remove from heat and stir in the chocolate pieces until melted and smooth. *Makes 1¼ cups.*

Put the sauce in a jelly jar and refrigerate until ready to give. Include instructions to reheat the sauce in the top of a double boiler and to serve it over very cold ice cream, which will make it crackle and become firm.

RUM-CHOCOLATE SAUCE

4 squares unsweetened
    chocolate
2 cups sugar
1 can (14½ ounces)
    evaporated milk

Dash of salt
1 tablespoon rum flavoring
    or 2 to 4 tablespoons
    rum

Melt the chocolate in the top part of a double boiler over boiling water; add the sugar, and mix. Add the milk and salt; stir. Cover, and cook over boiling water about ½ hour, or until hot. Beat until smooth. Cool, and add flavoring. Refrigerate. Good cold or reheated. *Makes about 3 cups.*

CUSTARD SAUCE

Custard sauce is a fine gift to accompany a variety of fruit desserts and plain cakes and puddings. It requires refrigeration, and thus should be given only when you do not have far to travel. We give three versions.

PLAIN CUSTARD SAUCE

¼ cup sugar
1 tablespoon cornstarch
¼ teaspoon salt

2 egg yolks or 1 whole egg
2 cups hot milk
1½ teaspoons vanilla extract

Mix the sugar, cornstarch, salt and egg in the top of a double boiler. Gradually add the milk, beating with a spoon. Cook over simmering water, stirring, for about 5 minutes, until slightly thickened. Remove from heat and stir in the vanilla. Chill. *Makes 2½ cups.*

CHOCOLATE CUSTARD SAUCE
2 squares (2 ounces) semisweet chocolate

Follow the recipe for Plain Custard Sauce, melting the chocolate in the milk.

BRANDY CUSTARD SAUCE
Follow the recipe for Plain Custard Sauce, omitting the vanilla and adding brandy to taste.

BROWN-SUGAR SYRUP

1 cup packed brown sugar
Dash of salt
¼ cup butter or margarine

½ cup water
¼ teaspoon vanilla extract
(optional)

Combine the sugar, salt and butter with the ½ cup water in a saucepan and cook for 3 or 4 minutes, or until thick. Add the vanilla. *Makes about 1¼ cups.*

Pack in gift containers and refrigerate until ready to give. Suggest serving it warm on waffles, pancakes or puddings.

HONEY SYRUP

2 cups sugar
1 cup honey

Juice of 1 lemon
2 cups water

Mix the sugar, honey and lemon juice with the water and simmer for 20 minutes. Give as a topping to be served warm over Greek Kataife (p. 134) or with waffles, pancakes or puddings. *Makes about 5 cups.*

FRUIT SYRUPS

Packed in hot, sterilized jars, these fruit syrups can be made at your leisure and given when an occasion arises. Suggest serving them on pancakes, waffles, puddings and ice cream or to flavor beverages.

APPLE SYRUP

1 cup apple juice
2 cups sugar

Cinnamon stick

Combine the apple juice, sugar and cinnamon stick and bring to a boil, stirring. Pour into hot, sterilized jars and seal. *Makes about 2 cups.*

RASPBERRY OR STRAWBERRY SYRUP

1 package (10 ounces) frozen raspberries or strawberries

2 cups sugar
½ cup water

Combine the berries, sugar and water. Bring to a boil, stirring. Skim off any foam with a metal spoon. Pour into hot, sterilized jars and seal. *Makes about 2 cups.*

ORANGE SYRUP

1 cup orange juice
2 cups sugar

2 tablespoons lemon juice

Combine the orange juice and sugar. Bring to a boil, stirring. Skim off any foam with a metal spoon. Add the lemon juice. Pour into hot, sterilized jars and seal. *Makes about 2 cups.*

GRAPE SYRUP

1 cup grape juice
2 cups sugar

1 tablespoon lemon juice

Combine the grape juice and sugar. Bring to a boil, stirring. Skim off any foam with a metal spoon. Add the lemon juice. Pour into hot, sterilized jars and seal. *Makes about 2 cups.*

GRAPE-ORANGE TOPPING

1 can (11 ounces) mandarin orange wedges	1 cup blue or red grapes, halved and pitted
1 teaspoon cornstarch	1 cup seedless green grapes
2 tablespoons sugar	

Puree the drained orange wedges in a blender. Combine them in a small saucepan with the cornstarch and the sugar. Bring to a boil, stirring. Simmer until thickened and translucent; cool. Pour over the combined grapes and toss to mix. *Makes 2½ cups.*

You can refrigerate this topping for a few days before giving it, if you wish. Suggest serving it on plain cheesecake, gingerbread, plain cake or ice cream.

BRANDY HARD SAUCE

1 cup sweet butter	1 teaspoon vanilla extract
2 cups confectioners' sugar	¼ cup brandy

Cream the butter and the sugar together. Beat in the vanilla and the brandy. *Makes about 3 cups.*

Give with English Plum Pudding (p. 136) or with Steamed Mincemeat Pudding (p. 134).

ORANGE-HONEY HARD SAUCE

3 cups confectioners' sugar
1 cup butter or margarine,
  softened

⅓ cup honey
2 teaspoons grated orange
  rind

Beat together the confectioners' sugar, butter, honey and orange rind until light and fluffy. Spoon into a decorative jar and refrigerate until ready to give. *Makes 2 cups.*
Give with Steamed Mincemeat Pudding (p. 134).

RUM HARD SAUCE

½ cup margarine, at room
  temperature
2 cups confectioners' sugar

3 tablespoons orange juice
  Grated rind of 1 orange
2 teaspoons rum flavoring

In a small mixing bowl, cream the margarine with an electric mixer until fluffy. Add the sugar alternately with combined juice, rind and flavoring, beginning and ending with the sugar. Beat until sugar is dissolved. *Makes about 2 cups.*
Put the sauce in a jar, ready for giving, and store in the refrigerator. Suggest serving it with steamed puddings or fruit pies. Or give it together with Steamed Mincemeat Pudding (p. 134) or Apple Pie with Cheddar-Cheese Pastry (p. 119).

LEMON-BUTTER DESSERT SAUCE

½ cup butter
1 cup sugar
1 teaspoon grated lemon
  rind

3 tablespoons lemon juice
1 egg, well beaten

Melt the butter in a heavy saucepan. Mix the sugar, lemon rind, lemon juice and egg and stir into the butter. Bring to a boil, stirring. *Makes about 1¾ cups.*

Pack in gift containers and refrigerate until ready to give. Suggest serving it warm on gingerbread, cake or pudding.

MELBA SAUCE

1 package (10 ounces)   ½ cup currant jelly
    frozen raspberries   ½ cup sugar

Combine the raspberries, jelly and sugar in a saucepan and bring to a boil. Simmer for 20 minutes, or until of desired thickness. Pour into a sterilized jar and seal. *Makes about 1 cup.*

When you give this sauce, suggest serving it on bread pudding, plain chocolate cake, cheesecake, fruit or berries. Or include it with a gift of Custard Rice Pudding (p. 137).

PEANUT-BUTTER TOPPING

1 cup dark corn syrup   Chopped peanuts
½ cup crunchy peanut butter   (optional)

Gradually add the corn syrup to the peanut butter, beating in an electric mixer or by hand. Additional chopped peanuts can be added, if desired. Store in a container with a tight-fitting lid. *Makes about 1½ cups.*

Give with instructions to heat before serving on baked custard, ice cream or pudding.

LEBANESE RAISIN-NUT SAUCE

1¾ cups light corn syrup
1 cup mixed light and dark
    seedless raisins

½ teaspoon cinnamon
Dash of salt
½ cup pine nuts

Mix the corn syrup and raisins in a saucepan. Bring to a boil and simmer 2 or 3 minutes. Remove from the heat and add the cinnamon, salt and pine nuts. *Makes 2 cups.*

Give with a tag suggesting that the sauce be served on vanilla pudding, pound cake or bread or rice pudding.

RUM CROCK

2½ cups drained canned
    fruits (diced peaches,
    pineapple chunks,
    mandarin oranges)
1 package (8 ounces) dried
    mixed fruits

¼ cup blanched whole
    almonds
2 cups superfine sugar
1½ cups dark rum

Layer the fruits, almonds and sugar in a 1½-quart crock. Gradually add the rum, moving fruit gently to dissolve sugar (rum should cover fruit). Cover crock and let stand 1 week or longer. *Makes about 1½ quarts.*

Give in pint jars and suggest serving the fruits on ice cream or crêpes.

TROPICAL TOPPING

1 can (6 ounces) thawed
frozen Hawaiian Punch
concentrate

1 can (8¼ ounces) crushed
pineapple, drained

Combine the Hawaiian punch and pineapple and stir well. Chill. *Makes 1½ cups.*

Include a tag with the gift suggesting that the topping be served on melon, fruit or berries. Or present it with a large, beautiful melon.

WALNUT SAUCE

1¼ cups packed light brown
sugar

1¼ cups water
½ cup chopped walnuts

In a saucepan, cook and stir the sugar and water until boiling. Boil gently, without stirring, 15 minutes. Add the nuts, bring to a boil and continue boiling gently 15 minutes. Cool and pour into jar. *Makes about 1¼ cups.*

This sauce is delicious with ice cream or plain cake. Give it with Sour-Cream Pound Cake (p. 84) or with Date-Graham Pudding (p. 132).

Candies and Confections

*H*OMEMADE CANDY is a delightful gift at any time of the year, perfect for children of all ages. These recipes include goodies like Cream-Cheese Fudge and Popcorn Balls for the very young and confections like Bourbon Balls and Pecan Pralines for more sophisticated palates.

It is best to make candy on dry, cool days; hot humid weather makes candies sticky and sugary. Candies will generally keep for about a week in a cool, dry place.

Invest in a candy thermometer. It's inexpensive, accurate, and you can also use it when you make jelly (see pp. 171–82). Don't let the bulb of the thermometer touch the bottom of the pot when you are reading it and remember to take the reading *before* removing it from the candy mixture. Check the thermometer's accuracy before using it: it should read 212° F. when heated in boiling water.

If you do not have a candy thermometer, you can test the temperature of the hot candy mixture by dropping a little of it into cold water and referring to the following chart:

Thread Stage	230°–234° F.
Soft-Ball Stage	234°–240° F.
Firm-Ball Stage	244°–248° F.
Hard-Ball Stage	250°–266° F.
Soft-Crack Stage	270°–290° F.
Hard-Crack Stage	300°–310° F.

Tips on Making Candy

- Use a very large, heavy pot so that the candy doesn't burn or boil over.
- Grease the candy pot with butter before starting to make the candy.
- To keep candy from sugaring, wrap a damp cloth around the end of a wooden spoon and use it to wipe out any sugar crystals that may form on the sides of the pot. Wash and dry all utensils thoroughly before putting them back into the candy mixture.
- Watch carefully, especially during the last minutes of cooking, to make sure candy doesn't burn.
- Cool candy on a buttered marble slab or heavy pottery platter.
- Store different kinds of candy separately.
- Most candies, with the exception of those made with fresh fruits, freeze well.

Ideas for Giving Candy

Candies look so cheerful wrapped individually in colored foil or plastic or poured directly into little foil cups made expressly for this purpose. You can also pack candies in clear plastic bags and tie them with heavy yarn, or use an interesting container which then becomes part of the gift—a candy dish, a flowerpot, a vase, a large brandy snifter or two, a pretty cannister or a glass apothecary jar. Young children will be thrilled to find candy in the back of a toy dump truck or in a little girl's straw basket.

You can make your own containers by saving nicely shaped boxes or coffee tins and painting them or covering them with self-adhesive paper. Foil pans or the plastic baskets in which berries and cherry tomatoes are sold make good containers for candy: line them with pink or purple tissue paper, fill them with candies, then wrap them in more tissue paper in a contrasting color.

If you wish, give a new candy thermometer along with your gift, or include some of the ingredients that were used in the candy—nuts, dried fruit or coconut, for example. You can also attach the candy recipe, always a thoughtful touch.

Charming old candy boxes can sometimes be found in antique stores or at barn sales. You can also make your own by decorating a tin or box with lace, hearts, doilies, old photos, or pressed flowers and leaves. The more thought that goes into the packaging, the more special the gift will be.

ALMOND-BRITTLE SQUARES

2½ cups sugar	1 teaspoon vanilla extract
1 cup finely chopped blanched almonds	¼ teaspoon salt

Heat the sugar in a heavy skillet (preferably iron) over medium heat, stirring constantly, until a golden syrup forms. Remove from heat and quickly stir in the remaining ingredients. Pour into a well-buttered 9-inch square pan. Let stand 2 minutes. With the point of a sharp knife, mark off in squares of desired size. Let stand until hard, then turn out and break into squares as marked. *Makes about 1½ pounds.*

APRICOT-GRANOLA CANDY

2 tablespoons butter or margarine, softened	1 cup finely chopped dried apricots
¼ cup light corn syrup	Natural cereal with raisins (granola type)
1 tablespoon water	
1 teaspoon vanilla extract	

Combine the butter, corn syrup, water and vanilla and blend well. Add the apricots and 2 cups of cereal and knead until well mixed. Moisten your hands with cold water and shape mixture into 1-inch balls. Roll in ½ cup of crushed cereal. Store airtight in a cool place. *Makes about 3 dozen.*

BASQUE SPHERES

2 egg yolks
3 tablespoons confectioners' sugar
½ cup plus 1½ tablespoons butter
2 tablespoons brandy

1 package (8 ounces) semi-sweet chocolate squares
Coarse decorators' sugar or finely diced toasted almonds

Beat the egg yolks with the confectioners' sugar until thick and light. Add ½ cup of softened butter and the brandy and beat in thoroughly. Coarsely grate 5 squares of the chocolate and fold in. Chill for 1 hour or until firm enough to handle.

Form into balls about 1 inch in diameter. Roll each in decorators' sugar or nuts to coat. Place on waxed paper.

Melt the remaining chocolate and butter over hot water in the top of a double boiler. Stir to blend and spoon over the tops of the sugared balls. Cool and set, then chill until ready to give. *Makes about 20.*

BOURBON BALLS

1 package (6 ounces) semi-sweet chocolate pieces
½ cup sugar
3 tablespoons light corn syrup
⅓ cup bourbon

1 package (7¼ ounces) vanilla wafers, finely crushed
1 cup finely chopped walnuts

Melt the chocolate in a double boiler over hot water; remove from heat and stir in the sugar, syrup and bourbon. In a mixing bowl, combine the wafer crumbs and walnuts. Stir into the chocolate mixture, blend well and immediately shape into 1-inch balls.

Store in an airtight container at least 1 week before serving. *Makes about 4½ dozen.*

BUTTERSCOTCH

2 cups sugar
⅔ cup dark corn syrup
¼ cup water

¼ cup light cream
¼ cup butter or margarine

Put all ingredients, except the butter, in a saucepan. Bring to a boil, stirring. Cook, stirring occasionally, until a small amount of mixture forms a hard ball when dropped in very cold water (260° F. on a candy thermometer). Add the butter and continue cooking, stirring, until a small amount of mixture separates in threads that are hard but not brittle when dropped in very cold water (280° F.). Pour into a buttered 8-inch square pan. When almost set, cut into squares. When cold, break apart. *Makes about 1¼ pounds.*

MOON BALLS

1 cup nonfat dry milk
½ cup honey
½ cup peanut butter

½ cup granola-type cereal,
    crushed

Mix the dry milk, honey and peanut butter together until well blended. Chill. Form into balls the size of marbles and roll in cereal. *Makes 3 dozen.*

CEREAL-PEANUT CRISP

5 cups unsweetened oat
    puffs or other crisp
    cereal
1 cup salted jumbo peanut
    halves

1 tablespoon butter
½ cup sugar
1 cup light molasses

Put the cereal and peanuts in a large metal bowl and heat in a very slow oven (250° F.) for about 10 minutes. Turn off heat. Or heat gently in a heavy skillet and transfer to a large bowl.

Put the butter, sugar and molasses in a heavy saucepan, bring to a boil and cook until a small amount of mixture forms a hard ball when dropped in cold water (262° F. on a candy thermometer). Pour over cereal and nuts and mix well. Turn out on a greased tray and let stand until hard. Then break into small pieces. *Makes about 1½ pounds.*

CHOCOLATE-DIPPED ALMONDS

2 cups whole almonds

2 ounces semisweet chocolate

Preheat the oven to 300° F.

Blanch the almonds in boiling water until the skins loosen. Remove the skins and toast the almonds on a cookie sheet in the oven for 10 to 15 minutes or until golden brown. Cool.

Melt the chocolate in the top of a double boiler over hot water. Hold each almond by the tip and dip the rounded end in the chocolate. Put on waxed paper on a tray. Chill until chocolate is firm. Store in a cool, dry place.

CHOCOLATE CARAMELS

3 cups packed light brown
  sugar
1½ cups molasses
¾ cup butter or margarine
3 tablespoons flour

6 squares unsweetened
  chocolate
1½ cups milk
1½ teaspoons vanilla extract
Almonds (optional)

Put the sugar, molasses, butter and flour in a pot and boil for 5 minutes. Add the chocolate and the milk. Cook, stirring frequently, until a small amount of the mixture forms a medium-hard ball when dropped in very cold water, or until the mixture registers 238° F. on a candy thermometer. Add the vanilla and pour into a buttered 9-inch square pan. Cool and cut into squares. Top each square with an almond, if you wish.

CHOCOLATE RAISIN CLUSTERS

12 ounces semisweet
  chocolate pieces or
  squares

1½ cups golden raisins
Plumped golden raisins
  (see Note)

Melt the chocolate in the top of a double boiler over hot, not boiling, water, stirring until smooth. Remove from heat, add un-plumped raisins and stir to coat with chocolate. With a small spoon, carefully make clusters in candy papers (if not available, put on a lightly greased baking sheet). Decorate each with a plumped raisin. Let harden in a cool place (not the refrigerator).

Note: To plump raisins, cover with hot water and let stand a few minutes, or until plumped. Drain and dry.

CHOCOLATE NUT FUDGE

2 ounces unsweetened
    chocolate
¾ cup milk
1 tablespoon light corn syrup
2 cups sugar
    Dash of salt

2 tablespoons butter or
    margarine
1 teaspoon vanilla extract
1 cup coarsely chopped
    walnuts or pecans

Combine the chocolate and milk in a heavy 2-quart saucepan. Put over low heat and cook, stirring, until smooth and blended. Add the corn syrup, sugar and salt and stir until the sugar is dissolved and the mixture boils. Continue boiling, without stirring, to 234° F. on a candy thermometer, or until a small amount of the mixture forms a soft ball when dropped in very cold water. Remove from heat. Add the butter and vanilla and cool, without stirring, to 110° F., or lukewarm.

Add the nuts and beat until the mixture begins to thicken and loses its gloss. Turn at once into a buttered 8 inch by 4-inch loaf pan. Cool at room temperature until firm, then cut into squares. *Makes 18 pieces.*

CHOCOLATE PECAN FUDGE

2½ cups sugar
1 jar (7½ ounces) marsh-
    mallow cream
¾ cup evaporated milk
¼ cup butter or margarine
1 package (12 ounces)
    semisweet chocolate
    pieces

½ cup chopped pecans
1 teaspoon vanilla extract
16 pecan halves

In a saucepan, combine the sugar, marshmallow, milk and butter; bring to a boil, stirring constantly, and continue to boil gently over medium heat 7 minutes. With a wooden spoon, beat in the chocolate, chopped pecans and vanilla until well blended. Pour into a greased 8-inch square pan. With the tip of a sharp knife, mark off 2-inch squares and press a pecan half in the center of each. When cooled, cut through fudge, rinsing knife frequently with hot water. *Makes 16.*

VIENNESE CHOCOLATE CONFECTION

2 cups ground, blanched almonds
1 cup grated, sweet cooking chocolate (about 1½ packages, 4 ounces each)
1 egg

½ cup sugar
½ cup finely diced citron
⅓ cup almonds, blanched and slivered
Superfine granulated sugar, white or colored

Combine the ground almonds and chocolate. Beat the egg and sugar until fluffy. Add to the almond-chocolate mixture, together with the citron and slivered almonds. Heat the mixture in the top of a double boiler over hot water until warm, stirring constantly until well blended. Cool.

Lightly spread a baking board or a sheet of waxed paper with sugar. Put the mixture on it and between sugared hands, shape into a sausage about 11 inches long. Roll in fine sugar. Dry in a cool place overnight. To serve, cut into thin slices. *Makes about 1½ pounds.*

CHRISTMAS JEWELS

½ cup peanut butter	1 teaspoon vanilla extract
½ cup honey	Red and green food
½ cup nonfat dry milk	coloring
granules	1⅓ cups flaked coconut
½ cup chopped dates	

Mix the peanut butter, honey, dry milk, dates and vanilla. Shape into about 3 dozen small ovals.

In 2 separate pint jars, put a few drops each of red and green coloring. Add ½ teaspoon of water to each. Put half the coconut in each jar. Cover and shake until the coconut is tinted. Roll ovals in coconut. Chill. *Makes 36.*

CREAM-CHEESE FUDGE

2 packages (3 ounces each) cream cheese, softened	1 teaspoon vanilla extract
2 tablespoons cream or milk	1 teaspoon rum
	Dash of salt
4 cups confectioners' sugar	1½ cups chopped pecans or
4 squares (4 ounces) unsweetened chocolate, melted	walnuts, divided

Beat the cheese and cream until smooth. Gradually beat in the sugar, then blend in the chocolate. Stir in the vanilla, rum, salt and 1 cup of nuts. Press into a lightly greased, 8-inch square pan and cover the top with the remaining nuts. Mark in 64 pieces about 1-inch square and chill until firm enough to cut (takes about 15 minutes). *Makes 1 pound.*

COCONUT-POTATO DROPS

1 medium-sized potato,
  peeled
1 teaspoon butter or
  margarine
½ teaspoon almond extract

1 package (1 pound)
  confectioners' sugar
1 package (7 ounces) flaked
  coconut
Cherries and nuts

In a small saucepan, cook the potato in water to cover until tender; drain and mash. Measure ½ cup into a bowl and stir in the butter and almond extract. Gradually stir in the sugar (mixture will be thin at first). Mix until smooth, then stir in the coconut. Drop by teaspoonfuls onto waxed paper. Top each with a cut candied cherry or nut. When cold, pack in an airtight container. *Makes about 45.*

COCONUT ALMOND-PASTE LOG

EASY ALMOND PASTE

1 can (8 ounces) pure
  almond paste

¼ cup light corn syrup
1 cup confectioners' sugar

COCONUT LOG

2 tablespoons light rum
2 tablespoons unsweetened
  cocoa

1½ cups flaked coconut

Make Easy Almond Paste by kneading the canned almond paste, corn syrup and confectioners' sugar together with your hands until well blended. Wrap in plastic wrap and store in a cool place. *Makes about ½ pound.*

To make the Coconut Almond-Paste Log, add the rum, cocoa and 1 cup of the coconut to 1 recipe of Easy Almond Paste and knead until well blended. Shape into 2 rolls, about 1¼ inches in diameter. Roll in additional coconut.

Wrap first in plastic wrap and then in foil. Store in a cool place. *Makes about 4 dozen ¼-inch slices.*

DATES STUFFED WITH ALMOND PASTE

½ recipe Easy Almond Paste (see p. 161)   1 to 2 pounds pitted dates
   Red, green or yellow food coloring

Add the food coloring, a drop at a time, to the almond paste. Knead with your hands until an even, pastel shade is attained. (You may need to coat your hands with a little confectioners' sugar while kneading.)

Shape the tinted almond paste into small balls, then into narrow strips slightly longer than the dates. Insert in the pitted dates and store in an airtight container in a cool place.

DATE-NUT SLICES

2 cups sugar
1 cup milk
2 packages (8 ounces each) pitted dates

Flaked coconut
½ cup chopped nuts

Put the sugar and milk in a heavy 2½-quart saucepan. Bring to a boil, stirring until the sugar is dissolved. Then cook, stirring occasionally, to 234° F. on a candy thermometer, or until a small amount of the mixture forms a soft ball when dropped in very cold water. Add dates and cook, stirring, 5 minutes, or until mixture is very thick and leaves sides of pan. Remove from heat and stir in 1 cup of coconut and the nuts. Turn out on a sheet of foil.

When the mixture is cool enough to handle and will hold its shape, roll up in the foil and chill 1 to 2 hours. Shape into 2 logs 9 inches long, roll in coconut and cut into ¼-inch slices. Wrap in plastic, then in foil, and store in a cool place. *Makes about 2¼ pounds.*

DRIED FRUIT BALLS

1 cup dried apricots	¾ cup confectioners' sugar
1 cup pitted dates	2 tablespoons orange juice or
1 cup seedless raisins	sherry
1 cup flaked coconut	Colored sugar

Chop the apricots, dates, raisins and coconut and mix together. Add the confectioners' sugar and the orange juice or sherry. Mix well and chill.

Shape into 1-inch balls, using confectioners' sugar on your hands if necessary. Roll in colored sugar.

Store in a cool place in a tightly covered container, putting waxed paper between the layers. *Makes about 50.*

FRUIT SAUSAGES

1 cup pecans	¼ cup candied cherries
1 cup shredded coconut	Grated rind of 1 orange
½ cup pitted dates	¼ teaspoon salt
½ cup seedless raisins	Finely chopped nuts
½ cup diced figs	
½ cup diced candied pineapple	

Grind the pecans, coconut, dates, raisins, figs, pineapple and cherries, using the coarse blade of a food grinder; add the orange rind and salt and mix well with your hands. Shape into rolls ¾ inch in diameter and 3 inches long. Roll in nuts and wrap each in plastic, tying ends with gold or colored cord. *Makes 16.*

HONEY-RUM BALLS

2 cups vanilla-wafer crumbs (about 7¼-ounce box)
½ cup rum

½ cup of honey
1 pound walnuts, ground
Confectioners' sugar

Mix the crumbs, rum, honey and walnuts, shape into balls and roll in confectioners' sugar. Store airtight for up to 6 weeks. *Makes about 5 dozen.*

FONDANT NUTS

UNCOOKED FONDANT
⅓ cup butter, softened
⅓ cup light corn syrup
½ teaspoon salt

1 teaspoon vanilla extract
1 pound confectioners' sugar

Red food coloring
Walnut halves
Green food coloring

½ cup toasted, chopped filberts
Whole filberts

Make Uncooked Fondant by combining the butter, corn syrup, salt, vanilla and confectioners' sugar in a large mixing bowl and kneading with your hands until well blended. If still sticky, add more confectioners' sugar until the mixture is easy to shape. Wrap in plastic and store in a cool place. Uncooked Fondant will keep for several weeks and can be used with many flavors and colorings. *Makes about 1⅓ pounds.*

Tint half of the Uncooked Fondant a delicate pink. Shape measuring teaspoonfuls of fondant into small balls, pressing a walnut half on each side. Store in an airtight container, with waxed paper between layers, in a cool place.

Tint the other half of the Uncooked Fondant a light green. Add the chopped filberts and mix well. Shape into ¾-inch balls. Put them in tiny foil cups, if you wish. Decorate each ball with lightly toasted whole filberts and store in an airtight container, with waxed paper between layers, in a cool place.

SUGARED NUTS

1 cup light brown or granulated sugar	Granulated sugar
2 cups maple syrup	Confectioners' sugar
1½ pounds (6 cups) pecans or other nuts	

In a heavy saucepan, combine the brown sugar and maple syrup. Bring to a boil and boil gently until a candy thermometer reaches 230° F., or the mixture spins a thread. Remove from heat and cool slightly.

Spread a layer of nuts in the bottom of a pie pan. Stirring nuts with a metal spoon, dribble enough syrup to coat. Repeat until all nuts are coated with syrup. Remove wet nuts to a pan of granulated sugar and stir until nuts are well covered. Then dust with confectioners' sugar. Dry in a cool place before packaging.

CHEWY ORANGE BARS

1 bottle (6 ounces) liquid
    pectin
½ teaspoon baking soda
1 cup sugar
1 cup light corn syrup
1 teaspoon grated orange
    rind
1½ teaspoons orange extract

¼ cup chopped candied
    orange peel
¼ cup finely chopped
    almonds
¼ cup grated (cookie) coco-
    nut or finely chopped
    shredded coconut
Additional coconut

Pour the pectin into a 2-quart saucepan and stir in the baking soda (pectin will foam). Mix the sugar and corn syrup in another saucepan. Place both pans over medium-high heat. Cook, stirring alternately, 3 to 5 minutes, or until foam disappears from the pectin and the sugar mixture is boiling rapidly. Pour pectin in a stream into the boiling sugar mixture, stirring. Boil, stirring, 1 minute.

Remove from heat and stir in the orange rind, orange extract, orange peel and chopped almonds. Sprinkle half the coconut on the bottom of a 9 by 5 by 3-inch loaf pan. Carefully spread the candy over the coconut in the pan and sprinkle with the remaining coconut. Refrigerate to harden. Cut into 2 inch by 1-inch bars and roll in additional coconut. *Makes 18 bars.*

PECAN PRALINES

3 cups packed light brown
    sugar
1 cup milk
¼ teaspoon cream of tartar
⅛ teaspoon salt

2 tablespoons butter or
    margarine
1 teaspoon vanilla extract
2¼ cups pecan halves

In a heavy saucepan, cook and stir the sugar, milk, cream of tartar and salt over low heat until the sugar is dissolved. Continue cooking, without stirring, to soft-ball stage (236° F. on a candy thermometer); cool to warm (110° F.).

Beat in the butter, vanilla and pecans until creamy; drop from a large spoon onto waxed paper and let stand until firm. *Makes about 24.*

PEANUT-BUTTER CHOCOLATE

12 ounces semisweet chocolate pieces
2 squares unsweetened chocolate

½ teaspoon salt
1 teaspoon vanilla extract
1 cup crunchy peanut butter

Melt all the chocolate in the top of a double boiler over boiling water. Turn off heat and add the salt, vanilla and peanut butter. Mix well and spread in a buttered 8 by 8 by 2-inch pan. Refrigerate for about an hour until firm. Cut into squares. *Makes 3 dozen squares.*

POPCORN BALLS

4 quarts popped corn
2 cups coarsely chopped pecans
1 cup butter or margarine

1⅓ cups granulated sugar
½ cup light corn syrup
1 teaspoon vanilla extract

Mix the popped corn and the pecans in a 6-quart mixing bowl. Melt the butter in a small saucepan and add the sugar and corn syrup. Bring to a boil, stirring, and simmer for 3 minutes. Add the vanilla and blend well. Pour over the popped corn and nuts, mixing constantly. Let stand 2 minutes to cool.

With your hands dampened in cold water, shape into 2½-inch balls and arrange on a baking sheet to set. Wrap each in plastic or foil and store in a cool, dry place. *Makes about 20.*

RICE-CEREAL CANDY

1 cup chopped nuts
3 cups puffed-rice cereal
½ cup butter or margarine
1½ cups light brown sugar,
 lightly packed

¼ cup light corn syrup
¼ teaspoon salt
2 teaspoons vanilla extract
 Red candied cherries
 (optional)

Preheat the oven to 325° F.

Put the nuts and cereal in a jelly-roll pan and toast in the oven, stirring occasionally, for 15 minutes. Transfer to a mixing bowl. Combine the butter, sugar, corn syrup and salt in a heavy saucepan. Bring to a boil over medium heat, stirring. Cook to 238° F. on a candy thermometer, or until a small amount of mixture forms a soft ball when dropped in ice water (check after 3 or 4 minutes of cooking). Add the vanilla, pour over the cereal-nut mixture and mix well. Cool a few minutes, then shape into 1-inch balls. Put on a baking sheet to harden and decorate each with a piece of cherry, if you wish.

Wrap individually with plastic wrap or foil. Store airtight in a cool, dry place. *Makes about 5 dozen.*

FRENCH TRUFFLES

1 package (8 ounces)
 unsweetened chocolate
1 package (4 ounces) sweet
 cooking chocolate

1 can (14 ounces) sweetened
 condensed milk
 Chopped pecans or walnuts
 or flaked coconut

Melt the chocolates together over hot water. Add the condensed milk and mix until smooth and blended. Cool a few minutes, then shape into balls, using about 1 teaspoonful of mixture for each. Roll in nuts. Store in an airtight container. *Makes 6 dozen.*

Jellies and Jams

*H*OMEMADE JELLIES and jams are always popular gifts and for good reasons. Served with freshly baked bread or rolls, they make a splendid breakfast or teatime feast. They are wonderful on crackers or in sandwiches, on ice cream and other desserts, or in trifles, cookies and cakes. Some jellies are also good with meat. There is no comparison between homemade preserves and commercial ones: homemade jams and jellies have less sugar, better texture, more fruit and more flavor.

Jellies and jams should be made when fruits and berries are in season. Neatly jarred and labeled, they are beautiful and decorative to have around, and you will always have something on hand for last-minute gift-giving.

You will need a large heavy pot, a ladle, jar tongs, a jelly bag or cheesecloth, jelly jars or vacuum-seal jars, paraffin and labels, as well as a water-bath canner for processing (see Pickles and Relishes, pp. 183–207). A jelly-candy thermometer is also handy.

Some fruits contain a lot of natural pectin and are cooked with sugar until they gel; others need bottled or powdered pectin, which takes less time to gel.

The jam or jelly should be poured while still boiling into hot, sterilized jelly jars with lids and sealed immediately. You can use ⅛ inch of melted paraffin to seal the jars. The paraffin should touch the sides of the jar all around, and any air bubbles in it should be pricked or they may become holes as the parafin hardens. Allow the paraffin to harden overnight before covering the jars with the lids.

If you plan to keep the jelly for a very long time, it may be better to use vacuum-seal mason jars. Ladle the boiling preserves into the hot, sterilized jar, filling it to ½ inch from the top. Wipe the rim with a clean, damp cloth and secure the lid and band tightly. Let the jar cool; a vacuum will form which will pull the lid down with a "pop."

Some of these recipes call for processing in a boiling-water bath. Indeed, many authorities these days recommend that all jellies and jams that are to be kept for any length of time be processed for 10 to 20 minutes, depending on the fruit. Certainly, if the jar doesn't seem to seal properly, you should give it a boiling-water bath to be sure. (See Pickles and Relishes, pp. 185–86.)

If jams and jellies are to be stored no more than 2 months, they do not need paraffin or a vacuum seal at all. Just cover the jars tightly and store them in the refrigerator. Many jellies and jams can also be frozen.

When making jelly, it is first necessary to let the juice drip through a damp jelly bag or a double layer of cheesecloth. This is a slow process, requiring patience. If you want the jelly to be absolutely clear, as it should be, don't squeeze the jelly bag.

Tips on Making Jellies and Jams

• It's best to cook small amounts of jam or jelly at a time.
• Follow the pectin directions exactly. Don't double recipes using pectin or the jams or jellies may not set.
• Prewarm sugar before adding it to jelly and it will keep the jelly from clouding.
• Test jelly with a candy thermometer (correct temperature is 220° F.) or put some in a cold, metal spoon and tip it so that the jelly runs off one side: if it slides in one sheet, without dripping or breaking, it is done. You can also test jelly by putting a small amount on a cold plate and letting it cool in the freezer for a few minutes; if it gels when cool, it is done. Remember to remove the pot of jelly from the heat while you are doing the testing.

• Stir jams well before putting them into jars so that the fruit doesn't rise to the surface.

• Melt paraffin in the top of a double boiler over warm, not boiling, water. Paraffin is very flammable, so watch it carefully.

• The finished jam or jelly may need a little time to set.

• It may take a few weeks to develop its full flavor.

• Jelly colors may fade if the jellies are kept too long or in a place that is too warm.

Ideas for Giving Jams and Jellies

A jar of beautifully colored jelly or jam makes a lovely gift without any decoration. Collect pretty jelly jars whenever you see them and have them on hand to sterilize and fill. You can tie them with ribbons in contrasting colors or wrap them in tissue paper, if you wish.

You may want to include a jelly spoon or a lidded jelly jar with your gift. Or give some home-baked bread or rolls (see Breads and Rolls, pp. 45–65) and some fine imported tea along with the jelly or jam.

APRICOT-PINEAPPLE MARMALADE

8 ounces dried apricots
1½ cups water
2 cups sugar
Grated rind and juice of
1 lemon

1 can (13¼ ounces)
crushed pineapple

Cut the apricots into small pieces with kitchen shears. Put in a saucepan with the 1½ cups of water. Bring slowly to a boil, cover and simmer 10 minutes.

Add the sugar, lemon rind and juice and pineapple; bring to a boil again and simmer uncovered, stirring occasionally, 30 to

40 minutes or until thick. Pour into hot, sterilized jars and seal. *Makes four ½-pint jars.*

CRANBERRY BUTTER

4 cups fresh or frozen cranberries	½ cup packed light brown sugar
2 cups water	Grated rind and juice of
2 cups granulated sugar	1 orange

Pick over the berries, rinse, bring to a boil with the water in a heavy 3-quart saucepan and cook until berries burst (about 10 minutes). Whirl in the blender until smooth, or force through a food mill. Return to the saucepan and stir in the sugars, rind and juice; bring to a boil and simmer, stirring frequently about 40 minutes, or until of spreading consistency. Pour at once into hot, sterilized jars, filling to within ½ inch of the top. Seal at once, then process in boiling-water bath 10 minutes. *Makes four ½-pint jars.*

CRANBERRY-ORANGE JELLY

1 quart cranberries	1 cup sugar
2 cups water	¾ cup honey
Grated rind of 1 orange	

Pick over the cranberries; wash and drain them. Put them in a saucepan with 2 cups of boiling water and the orange rind. Bring to a boil and simmer, covered, for 20 minutes. Force through a fine sieve or food mill.

Return mixture to saucepan and bring to a rapid boil; stir in the sugar and honey. Boil 3 minutes, then pour into hot, sterilized jelly glasses. Seal with paraffin. *Makes about four 6-ounce glasses.*

FROZEN SPICED GRAPE BUTTER

2 pounds ripe Concord
grapes
¼ teaspoon each ground
cloves and cinnamon

1¾ pounds (4 cups) sugar
2 tablespoons water
½ bottle liquid fruit pectin

Thoroughly crush the grapes, then work fruit through a food mill or press through a sieve. Measure 2 cups into a large bowl and stir in the spices. Add the sugar to the fruit and mix well. Mix the 2 tablespoons of water and the pectin in a small bowl. Stir into fruit mixture, then stir 3 minutes longer (there will be a few sugar crystals remaining). Ladle quickly into hot, sterilized glasses and cover with tight lids. Let stand at room temperature until set (may take up to 24 hours), then store in freezer. *Makes five ½-pint glasses or jars.*

If it is to be used within 2 to 3 weeks, the butter can be stored in the refrigerator.

JUNE JAM

3 cups shredded fresh
pineapple
2 cups cut fresh rhubarb
4 cups hulled, washed
strawberries

Dash of salt
4½ cups sugar

Put the pineapple in a large pot and cook without adding any liquid for 10 minutes. Add the rhubarb, strawberries and salt; cook 20 minutes. Add the sugar, bring to a boil and boil rapidly, stirring frequently for 25 to 30 minutes or until thick.

Skim off any foam and pour into hot, sterilized jars. Seal

with paraffin, cover with lids and store in a cool place. *Makes about six ½-pint jars.*

LIME MARMALADE

4 limes	5 cups sugar
⅛ teaspoon baking soda	Green food coloring
3 cups water	(optional)
1 box (1¾ ounces) powdered pectin	

Wash the limes, cut into quarters lengthwise and scrape out pulp and juice into a large saucepan. Discard the white membrane between the sections. In a separate pot, simmer the lime rinds with the baking soda and water to cover for 20 minutes. Drain and cool.

Scrape or cut all of the white part from the rinds. Cut the peel lengthwise into very thin slices with a sharp knife. Add the peel, 3 cups of water and the pectin to the pulp and juice in the saucepan. Over high heat, bring to a hard boil, stirring occasionally. Add sugar all at once, bring to a full rolling boil and boil hard, stirring, 1 minute. Remove from heat and add a little green food coloring, if desired. Let mixture set 7 minutes, skimming foam periodically. Pour into hot, sterilized jars and seal. *Makes six ½-pint jars.*

ORANGE-DATE CONSERVE

1 tablespoon grated orange rind	1 tablespoon lemon juice
1 cup orange juice	3 cups California dates
2 cups sugar	½ cup coarsely chopped walnuts or other nuts

Put the orange rind, orange juice, sugar and lemon juice in a kettle and heat, stirring, until sugar is dissolved. Then boil 10 minutes. Pit the dates and cut lengthwise into quarters. Add to the boiling syrup and cook slowly for 5 minutes. Add the walnuts and pour at once into hot, sterilized jars; seal. *Makes about four ½-pint jars.*

PEACH JAM

3 pounds ripe peaches	7½ cups sugar
¼ cup lemon juice	½ bottle fruit pectin

Peel and pit the peaches and grind or chop them very fine. Measure 4 cups into a large saucepan or kettle. Stir in the lemon juice and sugar. Put over high heat, bring to a full rolling boil and boil hard, stirring, for 1 minute. Remove from heat and at once stir in the pectin. Skim off foam with a metal spoon. Then, to prevent floating fruit, alternately stir and skim for 5 minutes. Ladle quickly into hot, sterilized, medium-sized glasses. Cover with ⅛ inch hot paraffin. *Makes about eleven ½-pint glasses or jars.*

SPICED PEACH AND BLUEBERRY JAM

4 pounds peaches	½ teaspoon salt
1 quart blueberries	2 sticks cinnamon
½ cup water	1 teaspoon whole cloves
5½ cups sugar	½ teaspoon whole allspice

Peel and pit the peaches. Force them through the coarse blade of a food chopper. Wash and pick over the berries. Combine with the peaches in a kettle; add the water and bring to a boil. Cover and simmer 10 minutes, stirring occasionally. Add the sugar and salt. Tie the spices in a cheesecloth bag; add. Bring to a boil slowly, stirring until the sugar dissolves. Boil rapidly for 10 minutes, or until fruit is clear. Remove the spice bag. Ladle into hot, sterilized glasses. Cover with ⅛ inch melted paraffin. *Makes eight 6-ounce glasses.*

PEAR HONEY

3 pounds (6 to 8 large) firm, ripe pears
1 cup undrained, canned, crushed pineapple

5 cups sugar
Red and yellow food coloring (optional)

Peel, core and slice the pears; force them through the fine blade of a food chopper. Combine with the pineapple and sugar in a kettle. Bring to a boil and simmer, uncovered, 20 minutes, or until thick, stirring frequently. Stir in a few drops each of red and yellow coloring, if desired. Ladle into hot, sterilized glasses. Cover with ⅛ inch melted paraffin. *Makes six 6-ounce glasses.*

· STRAWBERRY JAM

2 quarts ripe strawberries
¼ cup lemon juice

7 cups sugar
½ bottle fruit pectin

Crush the berries completely, one layer at a time. If desired, sieve half the pulp to remove some seed. Measure 3¾ cups of pulp into a very large saucepan or kettle. Add the lemon juice and sugar and mix well. Put over high heat, bring to a full rolling boil and boil hard, stirring, for 1 minute. Remove from heat and at once stir in the pectin. Skim off foam with a metal spoon. Then, to prevent floating fruit, alternately stir and skim for 5 minutes. Ladle into hot, sterilized, medium-sized glasses.

Cover at once with ⅛ inch hot paraffin. *Makes about ten ½-pint glasses.*

STRAWBERRY JELLY

2½ quarts fully ripe
    strawberries
¼ cup strained lemon juice

7½ cups sugar
1 bottle fruit pectin

Crush the berries, put in a jelly cloth or bag and squeeze out the juice. Measure 3¾ cups into a very large saucepan or kettle. Add the lemon juice and sugar and mix well. Put over high heat and bring to a boil, stirring. At once stir in the pectin. Then bring to a full rolling boil and boil hard, stirring, for 1 minute. Remove from heat, skim off foam with a metal spoon and pour quickly into hot, sterilized, medium-sized glasses. Cover at once with ⅛ inch hot paraffin. *Makes about eleven ½-pint glasses.*

TABASCO JELLY

2 teaspoons Tabasco (or
    more for a very hot
    jelly)
⅓ cup lemon juice

3 cups sugar
1 cup water
½ bottle fruit pectin
Red food coloring

Mix the Tabasco, lemon juice and sugar with 1 cup of water in a saucepan. Bring to a boil, stirring. Add the pectin and a few drops of food coloring, stirring well, until mixture comes to a full rolling boil. Boil hard for half a minute. Remove from heat; skim. Pour into hot, sterilized glasses and seal with paraffin. *Makes four 5-ounce glasses.*

TOMATO JAM

2¼ pounds ripe tomatoes	¼ cup lemon juice
1½ teaspoons grated lemon rind	6 cups sugar
	1 bottle fruit pectin

Scald, peel and chop the tomatoes. Bring to a boil and simmer 10 minutes. Measure 3 cups into a large saucepan or kettle. Add the lemon rind, lemon juice and sugar and mix well. Put over high heat, bring to a full rolling boil and boil hard, stirring, for 1 minute. Remove from heat and at once stir in the pectin. Skim off foam with a metal spoon. Then, to prevent floating fruit, alternately stir and skim for 5 minutes. Ladle quickly into hot, sterilized medium glasses. Cover at once with ⅛ inch hot paraffin. *Makes about nine ½-pint glasses.*

WINE JELLY

2 cups full-flavored wine such as ruby or tawny port	3 cups sugar
	½ bottle fruit pectin

Mix the wine and sugar in the top part of a double boiler. Put over boiling water and stir until the sugar is dissolved. Remove from heat and at once stir in the pectin. Pour into hot, sterilized, medium-sized glasses. Cover at once with ⅛ inch hot paraffin. *Makes about five ½-pint glasses.*

Pickles and Relishes

PICKLES AND RELISHES are wonderfully versatile: they are good as snacks, with sandwiches, as hors d'oeuvres, on a relish or antipasto platter, or as accompaniments to meat fish, poultry or eggs. They can also be used to flavor cold salads or to season bland dishes. They make infinitely useful gifts.

Some of these pickles and relishes will keep in the refrigerator or in the freezer. Most, however, should be processed in canning jars. Whatever the method of preserving them, homemade pickles and relishes bear little resemblance to their commercial counterparts.

Canning is the method we prefer, a technique that goes back to the traditions of our colonial ancestors. What a secure feeling to know that your pantry shelves are full of sparkling jars of homemade relishes, pickles, chutneys, and preserves, ready for your own use and for gift-giving throughout the year!

Homemade pickles are thrifty gifts. If you do your preserving when fruits and vegetables are in season, they will be abundant, at their prime and cheaper than at other times of the year. It's a great way to use the overflow from your vegetable garden. There are recipes here for things to pickle throughout the year, although the major activity comes in the summer and the fall.

A water-bath canner is necessary to process many of the acid fruits and brined vegetables for which we give recipes. Buy one intended for this purpose, or use a large pot with a tight-fitting cover, deep enough to cover the jars with at least one inch of water and fitted with a rack at least ½ inch from the bottom through which water can circulate. You can buy a separate canning rack to fit your own large pot. You will also need a large, heavy pot for cooking, a ladle, jar tongs, canning jars, lids, screw bands and labels.

Tips on Canning Pickles and Relishes

• Choose fresh, young, tender vegetables and ripe or slightly underripe fruits as free as possible from blemishes. Wash them thoroughly and remove any bad spots.
• Use a good grade of vinegar, one with four to six percent acidity. If the vinegar is too weak, the pickles will spoil or become soft. Use the kind of vinegar called for in the recipes.
• Follow the recipes as given. Don't double them, unless indicated.
• Be sure that jars are free from nicks or cracks and that lids are not rusty or bent. Wash them well and sterilize them in boiling water for 15 minutes before using them. Let them sit in the hot water until you are ready to use them. Follow the manufacturer's instructions for washing, sterilizing and securing lids.
• Fill jars to ½ inch from the top unless otherwise indicated.
• Run a long spatula between the inside of the jar and the contents to release any trapped air.
• Wipe rims clean with a hot, damp cloth so that the seal will be tight. If using lids and screw bands, put the bands on tightly. Follow the manufacturer's directions for other types of canning jars.
• Put the jars in boiling water as soon as possible after filling them. The water should cover them by at least one inch. They should not touch each other or the sides or bottom of the pot.
• Begin to time the processing period when the water comes to a boil again.
• Add more boiling water if the water evaporates during processing.
• When canning at high altitudes, remember that a longer processing time is required.

- Remove jars with jar tongs and let them cool on crumpled towels in a draft-free place.
- When they are cold, make sure that they are properly sealed and label them.
- Store them in a cool, dry place.
- Allow them to stand and develop flavor for at least 6 weeks before using or giving.

Ideas for Giving Pickles and Relishes

A glistening jar of homemade pickles or relish is a thing of beauty that requires no further adornment. Some like to decorate the lids of the jars, but this hardly seems necessary.

For special presents, you can depart from the standard vacuum-seal mason jar and pack your pickles in old-fashioned glass jars with rubber rings and wire closures. Some of these come with special designs embossed in the glass. Be sure to follow the manufacturer's instructions when filling and processing them.

If you wish, you can tie a fabric bow on the jar and attach some seasonal trimmings, such as a sprig of holly or some dried straw flowers. Or you can wrap the jar in tissue paper and tie it at the top with a ribbon.

Make sure the jar is labeled. The label itself can be festively decorated. If you wish, include the recipe for the pickle or relish and make some serving suggestions.

If you want to make the gift more elaborate, give several different kinds of relishes and some serving dishes or a relish tray. Or give several kinds of refrigerated relishes packed in matching pottery crocks.

APPLE CHUTNEY

1 pound dark brown sugar
2 cups cider vinegar
1 clove garlic, minced
⅓ cup thinly sliced
    crystallized ginger
2 tablespoons mustard seed
2 teaspoons ground cloves
¼ teaspoon cayenne
1 teaspoon salt
1 lemon, seeded and thinly
    sliced

½ cup raisins
1 cup water
¾ cup chopped green pepper
1 cup chopped onion
1 can (1 pound) tomatoes,
    drained well and
    chopped
4 cups chopped, peeled
    apples

Combine in a large saucepan the sugar, vinegar, garlic, ginger, mustard seed, cloves, cayenne, salt, lemon and raisins. Bring to a boil, then add the 1 cup of water and the green pepper, onion, tomatoes and apples. Bring to a boil again and simmer for 2 hours, or until thick and dark brown. Ladle into hot, sterilized jars to within ⅛ inch of the top and seal. Process in a boiling-water bath for 5 minutes. *Makes about seven ½-pint jars.*

SPICED CRAB APPLES

6 pounds (about 4 quarts)
    red crab apples
Whole cloves
4 cups cider vinegar
4 cups water

8 cups sugar
2 tablespoons broken
    cinnamon sticks
1 tablespoon whole allspice
Red food coloring

Wash the crab apples but do not remove the stems. Stick 2 or 3 cloves in each. Combine the vinegar, water, and the sugar in a large, heavy kettle. Tie the spices loosely in a cheesecloth bag and add it to the mixture. Bring to a boil and boil 10 minutes.

Add a few drops of food coloring and the crab apples, a few at a time. Simmer each batch 10 minutes, or until tender. Fill hot, sterilized jars with the apples. When all are cooked and packed, strain the syrup, bring to a boil and fill the jars to within ½ inch of the top. Seal tightly and process in a boiling-water bath for 20 minutes. *Makes four 1-pint jars.*

MARINATED BEANS

2 cans (20 ounces each) red kidney beans, drained and rinsed
2 cans (20 ounces each) chick-peas, drained and rinsed
⅔ cup diagonally cut green onions

⅔ cup slivered black olives
¼ cup pickled-pimiento strips
1 cup salad oil
¼ cup red-wine vinegar
1 tablespoon crushed coriander seed

Combine the kidney beans, chick-peas, green onions, olives and pimiento and stir gently. Mix the oil, vinegar and coriander seed together and pour over the bean mixture. Stir gently, and marinate in the refrigerator overnight. These beans will keep well in the refrigerator for 3 or 4 days before giving. Stir them occasionally. *Makes 12 servings.*

DILLED GREEN BEANS AND CARROTS

2 pounds green beans, washed and left whole or cut into 3-inch pieces
1 package (1 pound) carrots, peeled and cut into 3-inch strips
3 tablespoons salt

2 tablespoons mustard seed
2 teaspoons dillweed
  Crushed hot red pepper
  Dillseed
4 cloves garlic
2 cups white vinegar
⅓ cup sugar

Soak the beans and carrots in ice water to cover for about 30 minutes, then cook in 1 quart of boiling water with 1 tablespoon of salt for 5 minutes, or until of desired tenderness. Pack in 4 hot, sterilized pint jars. Put ½ teaspoon each of mustard seed and dillweed, a pinch each of crushed pepper and dillseed and 1 clove of garlic in each jar. Mix the remaining salt, the vinegar, sugar and 2 cups of water in a saucepan. Heat to boiling and pour over vegetables, filling to within ½ inch of the top. Seal and process in a boiling-water bath 5 minutes. *Makes four 1-pint jars.*

PICKLED BEETS

Small young beets	1 teaspoon each ground
Salt	cloves and allspice
2 cups sugar	1 tablespoon ground
2 cups strong white vinegar	cinnamon

Cook the beets in a small amount of boiling, salted water until tender. Drain, dip in cold water, then slip off skins. Put in a kettle. Mix 2 cups of water and the remaining ingredients and pour over beets. Bring to a boil and boil 10 minutes. Pack in hot, sterilized pint jars and fill to within ½ inch of the top. Seal and process in a boiling-water bath for 30 minutes. *Makes four or five 1-pint jars.*

RED CABBAGE RELISH

4 cups finely chopped red cabbage	1 tablespoon salt
1 small green pepper, finely chopped	½ to 1 teaspoon dry mustard
1 medium red or yellow onion, minced	⅛ teaspoon white pepper
	⅓ cup sugar
	⅓ cup cider vinegar

Combine the cabbage, green pepper and onion in a mixing bowl, sprinkle with the salt and let stand 1 hour.

Add the mustard, pepper, sugar and vinegar and mix well. Chill 1 hour. Keep covered, in the refrigerator for a few days, if you wish, before you give it. *Makes about 1 quart.*

SWEET CAULIFLOWER PICKLES

2 medium heads cauliflower
2 sweet red peppers, cut in strips
2 green peppers, cut in strips
1 quart onions, cut in wedges
1 quart white vinegar
2 cups sugar
½ cup light corn syrup
1 tablespoon each mustard seeds and celery seeds
1 teaspoon whole cloves
¼ teaspoon turmeric
2 tablespoons salt

Break the cauliflower into florets; there should be 2 quarts. Cook in a small amount of unsalted water 5 minutes; drain.

Combine the red and green peppers, onions, vinegar, sugar, corn syrup, mustard and celery seed, cloves, turmeric and salt. Bring to a boil, add the cauliflower and simmer for 2 minutes. Pack in hot, sterilized pint jars and seal. Process in a boiling-water bath 5 minutes. *Makes six 1-pint jars.*

CHILI SAUCE

4 quarts chopped, peeled, ripe tomatoes (about 6½ pounds)
2 cups chopped onion
2 cups chopped sweet red pepper
1 hot pepper, chopped
1 teaspoon ground ginger
1 teaspoon ground nutmeg
2 tablespoons celery seeds
1 tablespoon mustard seeds
1 bay leaf
1 teaspoon whole cloves
2 tablespoons crushed cinnamon stick
1 cup brown sugar, packed
3 cups white vinegar
2 tablespoons salt

Combine in a large pot the tomatoes, onion, sweet pepper, hot pepper, ginger and nutmeg. Tie the celery seed, mustard seed, bay leaf, cloves and cinnamon stick in a cheesecloth bag and add to the pot with the first mixture. Bring to a boil and cook, uncovered, until the mixture is reduced by half; stir frequently while cooking. Add the sugar, vinegar and salt and simmer 5 minutes more, stirring. Remove the spice bag, pack in hot, sterilized pint jars and seal. Process in a boiling-water bath 5 minutes. *Makes six 1-pint jars.*

SOUTH CAROLINA CHOWCHOW

3 pounds green tomatoes	2 cups sugar
6 firm, ripe apples	2 tablespoons mixed pickling
3 medium-sized onions	spice
2 sweet red peppers	1 tablespoon dry mustard
3 sweet green peppers	1 tablespoon salt
3 cups white vinegar	1 teaspoon celery seeds

Chop the tomatoes, apples, onions and red and green peppers very fine or force them through a food chopper, using a medium blade. Put the chopped mixture in a large kettle and add the vinegar, sugar, pickling spice, mustard, salt and celery seed. Mix well, bring to a boil and simmer, stirring occasionally, for 15 minutes, or until apples are tender. Pour into hot, sterilized jars and seal. Process in a boiling-water bath 5 minutes. *Makes four 1-pint jars.*

CORN RELISH

1 quart corn, cut from cob
  and cooked
1 cup finely chopped
  cabbage
1 green pepper, chopped
1 cup sugar
½ cup corn cooking water
2 cups white vinegar

1½ teaspoons celery seed
1½ teaspoons whole mixed
  pickling spices
2 tablespoons salt
1 tablespoon dry mustard
1 canned pimiento,
  chopped

Combine all ingredients, except the pimiento, in a kettle; bring to a boil and simmer, uncovered, 30 minutes, stirring occasionally. Add the pimiento, and pack into hot, sterilized ½-pint jars to within ¼ inch of the top. Seal and process in a boiling-water bath 20 minutes. *Makes five ½-pint jars.*

QUICK CORN RELISH

1⅓ cups cooked, whole-kernel
  corn
½ cup finely diced celery
1 tablespoon chopped
  green pepper
3 tablespoons wine vinegar

2 tablespoons brown sugar
½ teaspoon salt
⅛ teaspoon each pepper and
  turmeric
1 tablespoon chopped,
  canned pimiento

Combine all ingredients, except the pimiento, in a saucepan and mix well. Heat thoroughly. Add the pimiento. Cool and refrigerate. *Makes 2 cups.*

CRANBERRY-ORANGE-APPLE RELISH

1 pound cranberries	3 large tart apples
3 large oranges	2 cups sugar

Wash all fruit. Remove the seeds from the oranges. Core the apples and remove seeds. Force all fruit through the medium blade of the food chopper. Add the sugar, mix well and store in the refrigerator. *Makes about 7 cups.*

GINGER AND ORANGE CRANBERRY SAUCES

4 cups fresh or frozen cranberries	2 tablespoons minced crystallized ginger or
½ cup water	½ teaspoon ground
2 cups sugar	ginger
	Grated rind of 1 orange

Combine the cranberries with the ½ cup of water in a saucepan. Bring to a boil and simmer 10 minutes, or until berries pop. Pour into a mixing bowl, add the sugar and stir until cool.

Divide in half and flavor one part with ginger and one part with orange rind. Store, covered, in the refrigerator. *Makes about 1½ cups each.*

SWEET CUCUMBER RELISH

8 large, ripe cucumbers
¼ cup salt
4 sweet red peppers, seeded,
    cored
4 large onions, quartered

4½ teaspoons each celery
    seeds and mustard seeds
2½ cups sugar
1½ cups white vinegar

Peel and slice the cucumbers into a crock or glass bowl. Add the salt and mix well. Let stand overnight in the refrigerator.

Drain the cucumbers, then force them through the coarse blade of a food chopper with the peppers and onions. Put in a kettle; add remaining ingredients. Bring to a boil and cook, uncovered, stirring occasionally, about 30 minutes. Pack into hot, sterilized pint jars, seal, and process in a boiling-water bath 5 minutes. *Makes three 1-pint jars.*

SLICED CUCUMBER PICKLES

Pickling cucumbers
2 cups cider vinegar
½ teaspoon mustard seed
1 cup sugar
1 teaspoon mixed pickling
    spice

1 cup water
Salt
2 medium onions, sliced

Soak the cucumbers in cold water overnight; drain. Slice about ¼ inch thick with a serrated vegetable cutter. Bring the vinegar, mustard seed, sugar and pickling spice to a boil with the 1 cup of water. Add the cucumbers and boil 3 minutes, or until the cucumbers lose their green appearance. Pack the pickles into hot, sterilized pint jars. Add 1 teaspoon of salt and a few onion slices to each jar. Bring remaining syrup to a boil, pour over pickles and seal. Process in a boiling-water bath 5 minutes. *Makes three or four 1-pint jars.*

KOSHER-STYLE DILL PICKLES

30 to 36 cucumbers, 3 to 4 inches long	6 tablespoons salt
3 cups white vinegar	Fresh or dried dill
3 cups water	Garlic
	Mustard seed

Wash the cucumbers. Combine the vinegar, water and salt in a saucepan and bring to a boil. Put a generous layer of dill, ½ to 1 clove of garlic, sliced, and 1½ teaspoons of mustard seed in the bottom of each quart jar. Pack the cucumbers into the jars. When half filled, add another layer of dill and complete filling of jars. Fill to within ½ inch of the top with boiling brine. Seal and process in a boiling-water bath 15 minutes (pickles will shrivel some in processing but will plump later on standing). *Makes 2 1-quart jars.*

EAST INDIAN DATE CHUTNEY

2 cups cider vinegar	2 pounds dates, coarsely chopped
1 cup sugar	½ teaspoon cayenne
½ cup water	1½ teaspoons ginger
½ teaspoon instant minced garlic	¼ teaspoon salt

In a saucepan, mix the vinegar, sugar, water and garlic. Bring to a boil and cook for 3 minutes. Stir in the dates, cayenne, ginger and salt. Cook, stirring, for 5 to 10 minutes. Pack in hot, sterilized jars, seal, and process in a boiling-water bath for 5 minutes. *Makes 2 pints.*

SPICED FIGS

2 jars (17 ounces each)
   whole figs
1 cup packed light brown
   sugar

¾ cup white vinegar
1 teaspoon whole cloves
1 teaspoon ground allspice
2 sticks cinnamon

Drain the syrup from the figs and measure 1½ cups into a heavy saucepan. Add the sugar, vinegar, cloves, allspice and cinnamon, bring to a boil and boil 10 minutes. Add the figs and cook gently for 5 minutes, until heated. Pack in hot, sterilized jars, seal, and process in a boiling-water bath for 5 minutes. *Makes four ½-pint jars.*

PICKLED LEMONS

Large ripe limes can be used instead of lemons, if you wish, with superb results.

12 firm, unblemished lemons
   Coarse salt
   Paprika

½ cup olive oil
1 cup peanut oil

Scrub the lemons and slice them less than ¼ inch thick. Put the slices in a colander, sprinkle generously with coarse salt and let them drain about 12 hours. Turn after 12 hours, sprinkle the other side of the lemons with salt and continue to drain until very limp. Put the drained lemon slices in glass jars, sprinkling the layers with a little paprika as you put them in. Mix the olive and peanut oils and pour over the lemon slices to fill each jar to the brim. Cover and let mellow for about 3 weeks in a cool, dark place. Give with instructions to serve drained with roast chicken or pork, grilled fish or rice pilaf. *Makes four ½-pint jars.*

HOT MELON CHUTNEY

1 pint cider vinegar
1½ cups light brown sugar, packed
1 cinnamon stick
2 cardamom seeds
½ teaspoon aniseed
½ teaspoon coriander seeds
½ teaspoon mustard seeds
2 tablespoons salt
⅛ teaspoon cayenne
⅛ teaspoon mace

2 cloves garlic, minced
2 or 3 canned, hot green peppers, sliced
2 cups seedless raisins
¼ pound dried apricots, sliced
½ cup sliced preserved ginger
1 cup water
1½ pounds underripe melon

Mix the vinegar and sugar in a large pot. Add the cinnamon stick and the cardamom, anise, coriander and mustard seeds, tied together in a cheesecloth bag. Add the salt, cayenne, mace and garlic. Boil, uncovered, for 15 minutes.

Add the peppers, raisins, apricots, ginger and water and simmer, covered, for 30 minutes.

Peel the melon; discard the seeds and stringy parts and slice thin; measure 3 cups. Add to the pot and simmer, uncovered, for 45 minutes more, stirring occasionally. Remove the spice bag. Pack in hot, sterilized jars, seal, and process in a boiling-water bath for 5 minutes. *Makes five ½-pint jars.*

PICKLED OKRA

2 pounds tender fresh okra
5 pods hot red or green
    pepper or crushed,
    dried hot pepper
5 cloves garlic, peeled
3 cups white vinegar

6 tablespoons salt
1 tablespoon celery seed or
    mustard seed
    (optional)
1 cup water

Wash the okra and pack in 5 hot, sterilized pint jars. Put 1 pepper pod (or ⅛ teaspoon dried hot pepper) and 1 garlic clove in each jar. Bring to a boil the vinegar, salt, celery or mustard seed and water. Pour over the okra to within ½ inch of the top and seal. Process in a boiling-water bath 5 minutes. *Makes five 1-pint jars.*

PICKLED ONION RINGS

   Large sweet onions
2 cups white vinegar
1 cup sugar
1 teaspoon each mustard
    seed, celery seed and
    ground turmeric

¼ teaspoon powdered alum
   (buy in drugstore)

Peel and slice ⅛ inch thick enough onions to fill a wide-mouthed quart jar. Bring to a boil the vinegar, sugar, mustard seed, celery seed, turmeric and alum, and pour over the onions. Cool, then cover and refrigerate. Let stand several days before packing in smaller jars for giving. These onion rings will keep for several months in the refrigerator. *Makes 1 quart.*

GINGERED ORANGE OR GRAPEFRUIT PEEL

Peel of 3 large oranges or
  of 1 large grapefruit
1 cup sugar

2 teaspoons ground ginger
Ginger-flavored sugar

Cover the peel with cold water. Bring to a boil and cook until tender, pouring off the water and adding fresh cold water several times. Drain and cut the peel in thin strips with a scissors.

Mix the sugar and ginger in a saucepan, add ½ cup of water and cook until the syrup threads (242° F. on a candy thermometer). Add the peel and cook over low heat until the syrup is absorbed. Roll each strip in ginger-flavored sugar. Cool and pack in an airtight container. *Makes ½ pound.*

SPICED ORANGE PEEL

Soak the orange peel the night before you plan to cook it.

1 quart orange peel, cut
  into 2 by ½-inch strips
1¾ cups sugar

⅓ cup vinegar
1 tablespoon whole cloves
3 sticks cinnamon

Cover the peel with water and let stand in the refrigerator overnight.

Drain, put in a kettle and cover with water. Bring to a boil, drain and again cover with water. Bring again to a boil and drain. Cover with water, bring to a boil a third time and simmer 10 minutes, or until tender. Drain.

Put the sugar, vinegar, cloves and cinnamon sticks in a large pot and simmer 5 minutes to form a thick syrup. Add the peel and simmer, stirring frequently, 5 minutes. Pour into hot,

sterilized jars, seal, and process in a boiling-water bath 5 minutes. *Makes about three ½-pint jars.*

SPICED ORANGE WEDGES

6 medium-sized oranges	1 teaspoon whole cloves
2½ cups sugar	3 sticks cinnamon
¾ cup vinegar	2 cups water

Cover the oranges with water. Bring to a boil, and boil 20 minutes, or until quite tender. Drain, and cut into eighths. Combine the sugar, vinegar, cloves and cinnamon with the 2 cups
of water, stirring until the mixture boils. Add the orange pieces,
and simmer about 20 minutes. Pack into hot, sterilized jars, and
seal. Or cool, cover, and refrigerate; then pack in desired containers. *Makes about 3 pints.*

SPICED SECKEL PEARS

7 pounds seckel pears	1 cup water
6 cups sugar	1 tablespoon whole cloves
2 cups cider vinegar	Six 2-inch cinnamon sticks

Peel the pears but do not core or remove the stems. Mix the
sugar, vinegar and water in a large kettle and bring to a boil.
Tie the spices in a cheesecloth bag and add to the syrup. Simmer 30 minutes, then add pears and simmer until tender. Spoon
into hot, sterilized jars. Put lids on jars but do not tighten.
Boil syrup rapidly 30 minutes longer. Pour over pears to within
½ inch of the top. Seal and process in a boiling-water bath for
20 minutes. *Makes five or six ½-pint jars.*

PEAR CHUTNEY

4 to 5 medium-sized cooking pears
½ cup finely chopped fresh gingerroot
2 large cloves garlic, minced
1½ cups coarsely chopped onion
½ cup golden raisins
½ cup seedless dark raisins
¾ cup frozen lemon juice
3½ cups sugar
1 cup cider vinegar
¼ cup Worcestershire sauce
¼ teaspoon crushed red chili pepper
⅛ teaspoon hot pepper sauce

Peel the pears, cut each into 8 wedges, remove the cores and seeds and cut crosswise into ¼-inch chips. Measure 3½ cups of pear chips.

Combine the pear chips with the gingerroot, garlic, onion, gold and dark raisins, lemon juice, sugar, vinegar, Worcestershire sauce, chili pepper and pepper sauce in a heavy, 3-quart saucepan. Bring to a boil, reduce the heat and simmer uncovered, stirring occasionally, 45 minutes, or until thick. The pears should be translucent. Pour into hot, sterilized jars, seal, and process in a boiling-water bath 5 minutes. *Makes about four ½-pint jars.*

PLUM SAUCE

This is Chinese duck sauce, good with roast duck and most other meats and, of course, with Chinese food.

1 can (1 pound, 13 ounces) purple plums
¾ cup crushed pineapple, drained
1 medium-sized apple, diced
1 can (4 ounces) pimientos, drained
½ cup white vinegar
½ cup sugar
¼ teaspoon salt

Drain the plums, reserving 1 cup of syrup. Remove stones from the plums and put the fruit with the reserved syrup in a saucepan. Add the pineapple, apple, pimientos, vinegar, sugar and salt and simmer for about 1 hour. Force through a coarse sieve or a food mill. Keep refrigerated until ready to give. *Makes about 2 cups.*

PRUNE-WALNUT CONSERVE

4 lemons, thinly sliced
4 cups water
2 cups sugar
1 package (12 ounces) pitted prunes, each cut in half

1¼ cups coarsely chopped walnuts
¼ to ½ teaspoon nutmeg
¼ cup port

Cook the lemon slices, uncovered, in the 4 cups of water for 20 minutes, or until slices are tender. Drain off the liquid and measure (you will need 3 cups; add water if necessary to make up the amount). Put back in the saucepan with the lemon slices, and add the sugar and prunes. Cook over medium heat, stirring occasionally, 30 minutes, or until liquid is lightly syrupy. Remove from heat and stir in the walnuts, nutmeg and port. Pack at once into hot, sterilized jars, seal, and process in a boiling-water bath 5 minutes. *Makes six ½-pint jars.*

GINGER-TOMATO CONSERVE

1¼ pounds (1 quart) yellow or red tomatoes
2⅔ cups sugar
Grated rind 1 lemon
1 tablespoon chopped candied ginger or 1 piece whole dried ginger

1 teaspoon whole cloves
1 tablespoon lemon juice

Core the tomatoes and prick several times with a fork. Heat the tomatoes and sugar slowly with the lemon rind, ginger and cloves until the sugar dissolves. Bring to a boil and simmer, uncovered, for 20 minutes, or until thick. Add lemon juice and stir, then pour into hot, sterilized 6-ounce glasses. Cover with ⅛ inch of melted paraffin. (See Jellies and Jams, p. 173.) *Makes three 6-ounce glasses.*

GREEN TOMATO PICKLE

4 quarts thinly sliced green
    tomatoes
1 quart thinly sliced onion
⅓ cup salt
3 cups white vinegar
1 teaspoon whole allspice
1 tablespoon black
    peppercorns

1 teaspoon celery seed
1 tablespoon mustard seed
⅛ teaspoon cayenne
1 lemon, thinly sliced
3 cups packed brown sugar

Put the tomatoes and onion in a large bowl and sprinkle with the salt. Cover and let stand overnight; drain. Bring remaining ingredients to a boil and add the tomatoes and onion. Bring to a boil and simmer, stirring gently several times, about 10 minutes. Pour into hot, sterilized pint jars; seal. Process in a boiling-water bath for 5 minutes. *Makes five 1-pint jars.*

GREEN TOMATO RELISH

2 quarts chopped green
    tomatoes (4 to 5
    pounds)
2 medium-sized onions,
    chopped
2 quarts cold water
½ cup salt
1½ cups white vinegar

½ cup boiling water
1½ cups sugar
1½ teaspoons celery seed
1 tablespoon mustard seed
½ teaspoon turmeric
½ teaspoon cinnamon
¼ teaspoon dry mustard

Combine the tomatoes and onions in a crock or bowl with the water and salt; soak 3 hours. Drain and rinse thoroughly with cold water and set aside. Combine the remaining ingredients and boil 3 minutes. Add the tomatoes and onions, bring to a boil and simmer, uncovered, 10 minutes. Pack in hot, sterilized ½-pint jars, seal, and process in a boiling-water bath for 5 minutes. *Makes four or five ½-pint jars.*

INDIAN TOMATO CHUTNEY

2 pounds tomatoes
1½ cups sugar
1 cup cider vinegar
1 teaspoon instant minced garlic

1 teaspoon salt
¼ teaspoon crushed red pepper
1 teaspoon ground ginger

Wash, peel and cut the tomatoes into eighths. Combine with the sugar, vinegar, garlic, salt and red pepper in a saucepan; cook, uncovered, until syrup thickens and tomatoes are soft, about 45 minutes. Add the ginger and cook 5 minutes. Pour into a container, cover and refrigerate. *Makes about 1 pint.*

TOMATO-PEAR CHUTNEY

1 pound tomatoes, peeled and coarsely chopped
1 pound firm pears, peeled and chopped
1 green pepper, chopped
1 onion, chopped
⅛ teaspoon cayenne

½ teaspoon dry mustard
½ teaspoon ground ginger
1 teaspoon salt
½ cup cider vinegar
1 cup sugar
1 small pimiento, chopped

Mix all ingredients, except the pimiento. Simmer, stirring frequently, about 1 hour. Add the pimiento, pour into hot, sterilized jars and seal. Process in a boiling-water bath 5 minutes. *Makes about three ½-pint jars.*

TOMATO BUTTER

4 pounds (about 12) ripe
   tomatoes
2½ cups light brown sugar,
   packed

1¼ teaspoons cinnamon
1¼ teaspoons ground cloves
¼ teaspoon ground allspice
Dash salt

Scald, peel and quarter the tomatoes. Cook, covered, until mushy, stirring occasionally. Measure; there should be 1½ quarts.

Put back in pot and add the sugar, cinnamon, cloves, allspice and salt. Bring to a boil and simmer uncovered, stirring frequently, for 45 minutes or until thick. Fill hot, sterilized ½-pint jars and seal. *Makes four ½-pint jars.*

Give with the suggestion that the tomato butter be used on hamburgers.

MINTED WATERMELON PICKLES

Prepare the watermelon rind the night before you plan to cook it.

6 cups sliced watermelon
   rind (see below)
2 tablespoons salt
1 cup fresh mint leaves
2 teaspoons whole cloves

2 sticks cinnamon
3½ cups water
6 cups sugar
1 cup cider vinegar
1 lemon, very thinly sliced

To prepare the melon rind, peel off the green skin and cut rind in slices about 1¼ inches long and ¼ inch thick, leaving about ¼ inch of red meat on slices. Put in a bowl and cover with water mixed with the salt. Next day, drain the rind and cover with fresh water. Bring to a boil and simmer 30 minutes; drain again and set aside. Tie the mint leaves and spices in a cheesecloth bag and put in a kettle with the 3½ cups of water. Bring to a boil and boil 3 minutes. Stir in the sugar and vinegar. Add the lemon and melon rind and bring again to a boil. Simmer 45 minutes, or until rind is transparent. Pour into hot, sterilized ½-pint jars and seal. Process in a boiling-water bath for 5 minutes. Allow to age several weeks before giving. *Makes six ½-pint jars.*

ZUCCHINI PICKLES

2 pounds small zucchini	1 teaspoon celery seed
2 medium-sized onions	1 teaspoon turmeric
¼ cup salt	½ teaspoon dry mustard
1 pint white vinegar	1 teaspoon mustard seed
1 cup sugar	

Wash and cut unpeeled zucchini and peeled onions in very thin slices into a crock or bowl. Cover with water and add the salt. Let stand 1 hour; drain.

Mix the vinegar, sugar, celery seed, turmeric, mustard and mustard seed and bring to a boil. Pour over the zucchini and onion; let stand 1 hour. Bring to a boil and cook for 3 minutes. Pack in hot, sterilized pint jars and seal. Process in a boiling-water bath for 5 minutes. *Makes three 1-pint jars.*

Index

C

D

Q

R